"Mitton brings us on an exciting 14-day exploration of Celtic spirituality, each day starting with a well-told tale of a Brendan, a Patrick, a Brigid, or a Caedmon, followed by a Bible reading, wonderful modern-day questions, and Celtic prayers readers will want to make their own. What a gift for someone who might wonder if anything good can come from hinterlands!"

William Cleary
Author, *In God's Presence*

"*The Soul of Celtic Spirituality in the Lives of Its Saints* is a delightful description of Celtic spirituality. Each chapter provides an intriguing look at an important characteristic of Celtic Christianity that speaks powerfully to contemporary people today. This book, ideal for small faith communities, tells the stories of Celtic saints who loved God passionately and celebrated life fully. It is a must-read for anyone interested in Celtic spirituality."

Bridget Mary Meehan
Author, *God Delights in You*

"Through his appreciation of early Celtic faith, Mitton, an Anglican, reminds us that all Christians shared a common tradition before the Reformation, and that as Christians today, we benefit from the rich and diverse ways to God of all the Christian churches. The author leads us to ponder ways in which particular charisms of the Celts might be relevant to the spiritual quest today."

Dr. Elizabeth A. Dreyer
Washington Theological Union

"Mitton's approach is prayerful and pastoral. He not only writes a concise history of that earlier time, but invites the reader to reflect upon the meaning of that history for today. Lindsey Attwood's vibrant drawings add a rich symbolic dimension to the text. This book is for anyone who seeks to know more about the Celtic Christian spiritual heritage."

Edward Sellner
Author, *Wisdom of the Celtic Saints*

"There are basic principles behind the life of Celtic Christianity that make its spirituality applicable to an urban world. Michael Mitton has identified these principles and vividly illustrates each one as it applied in the lives of the Celtic saints. His book is an important step beyond historical nostalgia to restore balance and wholeness to the deeply fragmented world of Christian spirituality."

Rev. Jack W. Stapleton
Chaplain, The Order of St. Aidan (USA)

"Mitton is convinced that the approach to Christianity that distinguished our Celtic ancestors between the 5th and 11th centuries has much to teach us now. In this extremely readable and beautifully presented book he discusses 15 themes in the Celtic tradition."

Dr. Ian Bradley
The Church Times

"Mitton has done us all an immense favor in bringing us *The Soul of Celtic Spirituality*. The winsome power of the Celtic Church presents a profound and timely challenge to our modern Western expressions of Christianity. This book is about a period in history that is rich and fascinating. But it is equally a book that speaks strikingly to us today. We need to hear its message."

Rev. David R. Harper
Annandale, Virginia

"Mitton uses the stories of the Celtic saints—Brigid, Patrick, Aidan, David, Cuthbert, Columba and many others—to illustrate his thesis that the ancient Celtic Church has much to say to us today. He draws heavily from the Venerable Bede's accounts as well as from Celtic hymns and prayers. He recommends a return to the spirit and practices of the Celtic Church to invigorate the sort of Christianity that supplanted it. Easy to read and nicely illustrated."

Dr. John J. Young
University of North Carolina at Greensboro

"Mitton's is an imagination sensibly uncomfortable with the pat answers of the present and free enough to be thoroughly enchanted with the spiritual vibrancy of an earlier ancient Celtic accent."

Dr. Anthony J. Blasi
Tennessee State University

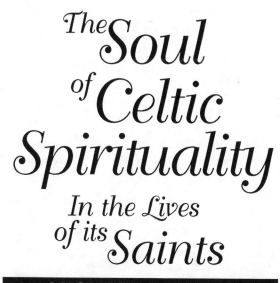

The Soul
of Celtic
Spirituality
In the Lives
of its Saints

MICHAEL MITTON

XXIII
TWENTY-THIRD PUBLICATIONS
Mystic, Connecticut 06355

North American Edition 1996

Originally published as *Restoring the Woven Cord* in England
by Darton Longman & Todd (140-142 Wandsworth High St.,
London SW18 4JJ).

Twenty-Third Publications
185 Willow Street
P.O. Box 180
Mystic, CT 06355
(203) 536-2611
800-321-0411

ISBN 0-89622-662-X
Library of Congress Catalog Card Number 95-60929
Printed in the U.S.A.

Dedication

To Julia, Russ, Carole, Jacqui, John, and Ray,
founders of St. Aidan Trust.

Thank you for your love for God,
your openness to the *Wild Goose*,
and for encouraging me to write this book.

Acknowledgments

Thank you to St. Aidan Trust for permission to use prayers from various liturgies.

For information about St. Aidan Trust and the Order of Aidan and Hilda, write to: St. Aidan Trust U.S.A., P.O. Box 4241, Evergreen, CO 80439.

Thank you to Lindsey Attwood for the drawings for this book. She has combined a remarkable talent with a deep appreciation of the Celtic way and a lovely openness to the Holy Spirit who has so clearly inspired her.

Contents

The Soul
of Celtic
Spirituality
In the Lives
of its Saints

Introduction

I n March of 1992 I set off on a journey that has changed the direction of my life. I traveled to the holy island of Lindisfarne which lies just south of the Scottish border, near Edinburgh. Here, during the course of two blustery wet and cold days, I became acquainted with this historic place, researching the lives of Aidan and Cuthbert who had lived here during the Christian dawn of the isles of Britain and Ireland. For me it was like a homecoming. Something about the island and its history connected with a deep longing within me, and brought together many different strands of my own faith.

As I explored the Celtic faith of this ancient mission center, I discovered something that I had been searching for during the past twenty years, an expression of faith in which I could "own" the various strands that have become so important for me. I discovered a burning and evangelical love for the Bible; I discovered a depth of spiritual life and stillness; I discovered a radical commitment to the poor and to God's creation; and I discovered the most attractive expression of charismatic life that I had yet encountered. Not only this, but I felt connected with my roots for the first time.

But was this just something personal to me? Was my interest in Celtic Christianity just an odd quirk, an indication of mid-life crisis? During the course of the ensuing two years I started to speak publicly about Celtic Christianity and was reassured to discover a widespread and growing interest in this subject. I am now convinced that all this is much more than just an odd quirk. I am in no doubt that the Spirit of God is reminding us of the first expression of faith in these isles to give us inspiration for Christian ministry and mission today.

While it had many faults, I believe the early Celtic Church was the closest thing we have in our Christian history to a complete expression of faith in this country. After all, no other church has had such an impact on this land, steadily converting the country from druid-led paganism to Christianity. Extraordinarily, most of us have been brought up on the notion of the "Dark Ages," with the implication that not much happened of spiritual worth until the Reformation. Nothing could be further from the truth. For Britain the period from the fifth to ninth century should be seen as the "Light Ages," where arguably a light shone that has been brighter than any since.

There is of course a real danger of romanticizing the Celtic Church and overlooking its weaknesses. Also, we should not generalize too much, as there were variations within it. Personally I am more attracted to the Lindisfarne-based mission that began with Aidan than the Iona-based mission that started with Columba.

Christian Beginnings in Britain

When the Roman legions were in Britain, some were Christians, and we have evidence of a Christian presence in this land from the earliest times. In the Manchester Museum there is a pottery shard that is inscribed with an acrostic of the Lord's Prayer in Latin, which is dated at around 180 A.D. The second-century writer, Origen, refers to Christians in Britain, and, at the Council of Arles in 314 A.D., we even have mention of three British bishops. There is also the Glastonbury legend that Joseph of Arimithea visited Britain. The story goes that Joseph was a tin trader and made regular trips to the West Country of Britain to purchase tin. He knew Jesus as a child and brought him on one occasion to Cornwall, thus inspiring the likes of William Blake to wonder if those feet in ancient times walked upon England's green mountains. The story continues that following the death and resurrection of Jesus, Joseph traveled to England again, this time carrying the Holy Grail that carried the blood and sweat of Christ, arriving eventually at the Isle of Avalon, Glastonbury. While this story is usually viewed as quaint legend, it is not entirely implausible to believe that Joseph was a tin trader and, as such, would likely have made journeys to the tin-rich island of Britain. Gildas, the sixth-century historian, speaks of Britain receiving the "beams of light" of the gospel in the reign of Tiberias. Since Tiberias died in 37 A.D., this speaks of a very early mission indeed. We shall probably never know the truth of all this, but there certainly are hints in our history that the gospel arrived in Britain and Ireland during the period of the Acts of the Apostles.

The Christianity that came with the Roman legions seems to have had little effect on the local population, who preferred their indigenous pagan ways to the religion of the conquering forces. When Rome abandoned Britain in the early fifth century they took the Christian faith with them. What was left were the pockets of faith that were about to burst into the flame that we now call Celtic Christianity. This flourished, especially in the areas of the lands that the Romans had failed to occupy, in particular in Ireland, which was never conquered by the Romans. For a time this indigenous expression of Christian life was the only one that existed in Britain and Ireland, until the church in Western Europe, based in Rome, developed a concern for Britain. This concern developed because unevangelized tribes of Angles and Saxons were pouring into Britain, and also because the British Celtic Church was becoming wayward, partly due to its custom of following a different date of Easter from the Western Church. Thus Pope Gregory in Rome commissioned Bishop Augustine for his famous mission to the English. Augustine and his forty missionary monks arrived in the South of England in 597 A.D. and set up base at Canterbury. As we shall see from time to time in the pages of this book, the relationship between the British and Roman Church was an easy one. Both churches had strengths and weaknesses and were genuinely concerned about bringing the light of Christ to these lands, and there was room for both. But in time the Roman Church felt that there could only be room for one church, united in celebrating Easter on a common date with the rest of Western Europe, and it therefore sought to absorb the British Church into this wider network.

By the end of the sixth century, the Roman Church was flourishing in a collapsing, but generally Christian Empire. It seems that very soon after the conversion of the Roman Emperor Constantine in the fourth century, the Christian Church started to become extraordinarily worldly in stark contrast to the very vibrant and charismatic faith that had seen it through the terrible years of persecution under the emperors Diocletian and Galerius. Once it had become part of the establishment, it was inclined to espouse the values of the earthly kingdom rather than the kingdom of God.

By contrast, in the East, thousands were reacting strongly to this worldliness and nominalism and moved to the deserts, where, led by the likes of Anthony and Pachomius, they set up monasteries that became oases of spiritual life and wisdom. These were the first expressions of monastic life in the Christian Church. People were attracted to the wilderness because of the many biblical examples of desert journey, in particular that of Jesus after his baptism in the Jordan. The culmination of his forty-day ascetic life was a fierce contest with the devil. The desert monks and nuns felt similarly called to these hostile wastelands, which were graphic illustrations of the spiritual wasteland of nominalism and worldliness in the church. Here on behalf of the church, they did battle with Satan, pleading with God through prayer, fasting, and holiness to have mercy on the church and restore it for its mission to a needy world. Both religious communities and thousands of individual hermits played a key role in the spiritual survival of the church. Not only did they act as spiritual warriors, but they also modeled lives of commitment, depth, and transparent holiness.

Martin, Bishop of Tours (371 A.D.), was the first Westerner to become influenced by the Eastern monks, and he founded a monastery called Marmoutier, literally meaning "the place of the big family." It was here that the Scottish Ninian was profoundly influenced, and the story of the Celtic Church in Britain gets underway. With Ninian and Columba in Scotland; David, Samson, and Illtyd in Wales; Patrick and Brigid in Ireland; Aidan, Cuthbert, and Hilda in England (to name but a few), the Celtic fire began to blaze.

By the time the Roman mission arrived in Canterbury, the Celtic Church was looking to the East rather than the West for its inspiration. In fact, for a time the Roman mission was only effective in the South because the Midlands, the North, and the rest of Britain and Ireland were unreachable. This was due to the ravages of Anglo-Saxon invasions and the frequent outbreaks of plague. It was only with the settling down of the Saxons, that the Roman Church began to see the possibility of establishing "one" church in Britain that would celebrate one Easter. The Roman Church eventually persuaded Celtic leaders to gather for a synod where this could be thrashed out. Thus in 664 at Whitby, both sides met. Here the increasingly powerful Wilfrid, who was forming dioceses and monasteries based on Roman models, was far more competent at arguing his case than his typically humble Celtic opponents. It is not too dramatic to say that there the spiritual fate of the land was decided. The Celtic Church lost against the powers of Rome. The community-based church, which was committed to poverty, could not stand against the hierarchical and centrally organized church that had such effective links with secular power. But the Celtic fire still burned for many years following Whitby, and has remained alight in the "Celtic fringes" through the ages. Today it is showing every sign of being rekindled across the land, and indeed across the world.

The conflict just described was between Celt and Roman. But let me make it clear that, by "Roman Church," I am not referring to the modern-day Roman Catholic Church. I am talking about a church that existed a thousand years before the Reformation. The Roman Church of the Middle Ages influenced most of the Western Church, Catholic *and* Protestant. In this book I am interested in how the indigenous church of Britain and Ireland expressed its faith before it became absorbed into that wider Rome-based church.

Strands of Faith

The Celts were great lovers of art, and they loved intricate patterns. Such artwork can be found in the *Book of Kells* or the *Lindisfarne Gospels,* where the illuminations are based on wonderful and intricate strands that are interwoven to form the most beautiful patterns, full of vitality and meaning. You see the same in other expressions of Celtic Christian art that have survived to this day, such as the engraved high crosses in Ireland and parts of Britain, which were covered with these interwoven designs.

It is these patterns that represent so clearly the Celtic love of wholeness, and they say something very important to the church today about how the Celts lived their Christian lives. They discovered the many different strands of our faith and wove them together in a most effective cord for ministry and mission. A strong cord needs many strands, but the weakness of the church through the ages is that it has tended to focus on only one or two of these strands. Since the collapse of the Celtic Church, one religious group after another has discovered one of these lost strands and has mistaken it for the main cord, rather than weaving it in with the other strands. One strand, of course, never has sufficient strength. Examples of such "strands" include the evangelical discoveries of justification by faith at the Reformation; Catholic discoveries about worship and sacraments at the Oxford Movement last century; liberal discoveries about social justice and radical witness to the poor during this century; and pentecostal discoveries within the charismatic renewal in the second half of this century. All of these are good and necessary discoveries, but they are only part of the whole cord of faith. In the Celtic

Church there was a community of faith that was refreshingly free of prejudice, and that was open to welcoming many strands into the cord of faith.

We need to study the Celtic Church in the spirit in which its members lived out their Christian lives, with total openness to the wind of the Spirit, who may well draw our attention to strands of our Christian faith that we have too easily ignored or discarded. Too many are approaching the Celtic Church only interested in their own agendas. It would be all too easy for me, as someone who is closely involved in charismatic renewal, for example, to pick out the charismatic strands, and ignore some of the others that can challenge me to grow. We will need to explore with a great sense of openness.

My hope is that this book will help us to rediscover some of the very important strands of faith that were clearly evident in the Celtic Church. Of equal importance to the discovery is the weaving of them together in our personal walk with God and in the life of the church. I have not identified all the strands, but I have chosen fourteen that are important for us today. They are in alphabetical order, which I hope makes clear that there is no preference of one strand over another. Each chapter is simply a snapshot of the early Celtic Church to give you some idea of how it experienced this particular strand of Christian faith. (Note that though for many Christians today, in Cornwall, Wales, Ireland, and Scotland, the Celtic Church is not just in the past but is alive and well in the present. In this book I am referring to the early Celtic Church.)

It is my deep conviction that the Celtic Church challenges us to rediscover the strands of our faith and find ways of weaving them together in our personal lives and the life of the church. We need a strong cord with many strands, and we need the weaving to take place in our own lives.

To guide readers in this process, each chapter of this book has five components:

1) A story with extensive commentary. Story was very important to those in the Celtic Church. They taught through

stories, songs, poems, and pictures. Pre-Christian Celts actually had very little interest in writing, which is one reason why
it is difficult to do historical research about them. But they
were strong on oral tradition, and they delighted in storytelling, which they viewed as an imaginative way of communicating truth. Each of my chapters will have one leading
story about a "saint" from the Celtic Church, and I will use
this, along with various other stories, to discuss the theme of
the chapter. My primary resource for these stories is the
Venerable Bede, and this reflects my admiration for him. I
particularly love the early Celtic Church in Northumbria, so I
will regularly turn to stories from this church. Also, because
Bede wrote such a thorough account of Cuthbert's life, this
particular saint features more regularly in my stories than others. Only two female saints appear in my stories, simply because most available information is about male saints. This
certainly does not reflect the Celtic Church's estimation of
women, which was very high indeed.

2) Bible reading. There is a Bible reading in each chapter
that relates to the theme of the chapter. These will help readers to prepare for the application section.

3) Questions for reflection and discussion. This section contains questions to help readers apply the theme of the chapter
to their present situations. These questions can be used for
personal reflection, or as starter questions for group study.

4) A prayer. All the prayers in this book are kindly provided by the St. Aidan Trust, and are written either by Ray
Simpson or myself (apart from Columba's in Chapter 8).

5) An image. Each chapter has a drawing by Lindsey
Attwood. She drew them after prayerfully considering the
theme of each chapter, and they are offered as inspiration for
prayer and meditation—true to the Celtic way of hearing God
through picture as well as word.

Chapter 1

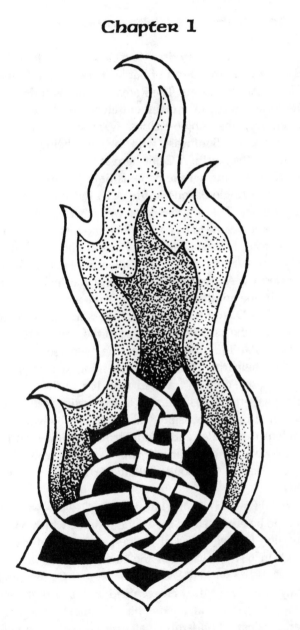

Authenticity, Simplicity, and Holiness

St. Aidan, Bishop of Lindisfarne

As the fifth century drew to a close, Britain found itself in a constant round of battles between the Celts and the Anglo-Saxons. The Roman armies withdrew leaving the locals to battle it out themselves. By the end of the sixth century, the Anglo-Saxons were in control of the Midlands and the Southeast, with the Celts being pushed to the West and the North. A Celtic hero at this time was the legendary King Arthur, whose name is linked with a great victory over the Anglo-Saxons in 516 A.D. But this victory was only temporary. The Anglo-Saxons were there to stay and, in time, the nation came to be named England after the Angles.

It was around this time that the Pope in Rome became concerned about evangelizing Anglo-Saxon Britain, and he sent a mission led by Augustine to evangelize the invading tribes gathered in the southeast of Britain. They arrived in Canterbury in 597 A.D. and, once settled, they were joined by other missionaries who assisted them. One of these was a bishop by the name of Paulinus, who later became the personal chaplain to Queen Ethelberga. She married the king of Northumbria, Edwin, and so Paulinus traveled with her to the Northeast. Despite great efforts, his attempts to evangelize were not successful. In time the mission was shattered by war. Kings Cadwallon from Wales and Penda from Mercia joined forces to invade Northumbria. King Edwin was killed in battle, and the Queen had to flee south, taking her chaplain, Paulinus, with her.

The royal family fled, and one of them, Oswald, was sent to Scotland to be educated on the Island of Iona, which had won a reputation for being one of the best places of education in the land. In 634, Oswald felt the time was right to rid his homeland of the wicked Cadwallon. He met Cadwallon and his army at a place called Heavenfield and, before the battle, he put a cross in the soil, making his Christian faith abundantly clear. Against all odds his small army defeated Cadwallon and he became king.

One of the first things he did was to send to Iona for a missionary. The Iona monastery at first sent Corman, a man of "austere disposition" who did not go down well with the English; and, after a while, Corman returned despondent to Iona, abandoning his mission and complaining that the English were an "ungovernable people of an obstinate and barbarous temperament!"

The community at Iona held a conference to work out what to do next. Present at this conference was an Irish monk called Aidan, who listened intently to Corman's report. He then rose and said to Corman, "Brother, it seems to me that you were too severe on your ignorant hearers. You should have followed the practice of the Apostles, and begun by giving them the milk of simpler teaching, and gradually nourished them with the word of God." When Aidan had finished speaking, the conference fell into silence and all eyes were on him. They sensed that there was a clear call of God on Aidan to go and evangelize the English, and so, without further ado, he was duly consecrated bishop and sent off with the prayers and blessings of the Iona monastery.

Aidan was consecrated in 635 and immediately traveled to Northumbria and met with King Oswald at Bamburgh on the Northumbrian Coast. A few miles up from Bamburgh lies the tidal island of Lindisfarne, and here Aidan formed a mission base of Christian people who were trained in teaching and evangelism. This was one of the most effective mission bases England has ever seen. Here Aidan stayed, overseeing his community, setting up other communities in the Northeast, and training people like Hilda, Chad, and his brothers.

Aidan's ministry in England is significant not so much for what he did, but more for the kind of person he was and for the kind of Christian spirituality and witness he modeled. This deeply impressed the British people and would affect the Celtic Church in England for several generations. The Venerable Bede writes of Aidan:

> Among other evidences of holy life, he gave his clergy an inspiring example of self-discipline and continence, and the highest recommendation of his teaching to all was that he and his followers lived as they taught. He never sought or cared for any worldly possessions, and loved to give away to the poor

who chanced to meet him whatever he received from kings or wealthy folk. Whether in town or country, he always traveled on foot unless compelled by necessity to ride; and whatever people he met on his walks, whether high or low, he stopped and spoke to them. If they were heathen, he urged them to be baptized; and if they were Christians, he strengthened their faith, and inspired them by word and deed to live a good life and to be generous to others. His life is in marked contrast to the apathy of our own times.[1]

Aidan's example was different from the model of Christianity then being expressed in the Western European Church, which had formed its center in Rome. By being so closely connected with the former Roman Empire, the church in Rome had uncritically espoused a number of secular values and ways of working. While the Celtic Church had its faults, its strength lay in the fact that it had never had much to do with powerful institutions, and it formed its life and witness among the poor and the insignificant. Thus there were in Britain in the seventh century two fairly contrasting expressions of Christian life.

Both Roman and Celtic Christianity were strongly community based, and for both the monasteries were very effective mission bases. But the styles of monastic life differed considerably. Magnus Magnusson describes these differences which in many ways summarized the cultural differences between these two expressions of Christianity:

> Celtic monks lived in conspicuous poverty; Roman monks lived well. Celtic monks were unworldly, Roman monks were worldly. Celtic bishops practiced humility; Roman bishops paraded pomp. Celtic bishops were ministers of their flocks; Roman bishops were monarchs of their dioceses. Celtic clergymen said, "Do as I do," and hoped to be followed; Roman clergymen said, "Do as I say," and expected to be obeyed.[2]

Some would say that this is an exaggeration of the differences, but certainly if you compare the Roman Wilfrid with the Celtic Aidan or Cuthbert, you do see very different approaches.

Consider the eighth-century *Life of Wilfrid* by Eddius Stephanus in relation to Bede's *Life of Cuthbert*. In Bede we hear stories of Cuthbert's austere hermitage on Farne Island and the simple lifestyle of the monks on Lindisfarne. By contrast, Wilfrid, himself originally trained on Lindisfarne, soon became attracted to the values of the Roman Empire. Thus, where Aidan and Cuthbert were content to build small wooden makeshift dwellings for their monks and nuns and erect simple churches, Wilfrid was planning far grander things, no doubt sincerely believing that it was in the interests of the gospel and the church to do so. One of Wilfrid's achievements was to build a fine church at Ripon.

According to Stephanus, Wilfrid "adorned the bridal chamber of the true Bridegroom and Bride with gold and silver and every shade of purple: At Ripon he started and completed from foundation to roofbeam a church built of dressed stone, supported with columns and complete with side aisles." This was how people were building churches in Europe, and this was seen to be appropriate for Britain. At the dedication of the church, "Wilfrid stood before the altar, facing the people, and in the kings' presence read out in a clear voice a list of lands which previous monarchs and now themselves had given him for their soul's salvation with the consent and signature of the bishops and all the earldom."[3] The dressed stone of Ripon was in stark contrast to the Celtic daub and wattle, and Wilfrid's interests in land possession would have been anathema to the Celtic bishops.

No doubt both approaches were sincere. The Celtic approach, however, was much more gentle and humble, and therefore altogether more sensitive to the people being evangelized. Aidan's gentle personality and spirituality were absolutely key to the mission. He was a man who had an infectious holiness which, far from making him remote and otherworldly, enabled him to mix with all kinds of people and to understand their world. They could believe in his message because he was a person whose lifestyle was transparently attractive to all who were seeking God. In Aidan we see the lifestyle of the Beatitudes very attractively displayed.

The Irish Aidan was no doubt deeply influenced by the likes of Brigid. Ian Bradley writes:

For all the legends about their miraculous deeds and supernatural powers, they also had a great simplicity and this is one
of their most attractive characteristics for us today. When St.
Brigid, abbess of the great mixed monastery at Kildare, was
asked what were the three things most pleasing to God, she replied, true faith in the Lord with a pure heart, a simple life
with piety, and generosity with charity. These were all qual-
ities that the Celtic saints exhibited very clearly in their own
lives.[4]

Concern for the Poor

This simple lifestyle meant that the Celtic Church had no difficulty in communicating with the poor. Indeed, it considered
concern for the poor a high priority. Bede tells us of Aidan:

> If wealthy people did wrong, he never kept silent out of re-
> spect or fear, but corrected them outspokenly. Nor would he
> offer money to influential people, although he offered them
> food whenever he entertained them as host. But, if the wealthy
> ever gave him gifts of money, he either distributed it for the
> needs of the poor, as I have mentioned, or else he used it to
> ransom any who had unjustly been sold as slaves. Many of
> those whom he had ransomed in this way later became his dis-
> ciples; and when they had been instructed and trained, he or-
> dained them to the priesthood.[5]

It is worth dwelling on the thought that the first theological
college in England included a large number of freed slaves.
Such people were clearly able to understand the poor of the
land. It is probably true to say that this was the one time in
history that the English Church genuinely lived close to the
people. Once it started investing in lands and properties and
building fine bridges, it inevitably began to distance itself
from the poor.

This choice to be poor was probably not an easy one. As we
have seen, Aidan, in his closeness to the royal family, would
have seen the pleasures that money could buy. We also get
the occasional insight that Cuthbert was tempted by wealth.
When the young Cuthbert became Prior of Melrose, Bede tells
us that Cuthbert would often lament: "If I could live in a tiny
dwelling on a rock in the ocean, surrounded by the swelling
waves, cut off from the knowledge and the sight of all, I

would still not be free from the cares of this fleeting world, or from the fear that somehow the love of money might snatch me away."[6]

His longing for solitude led him eventually to Farne Island, but he knew himself well enough to know that removal from the world would not stop his longing for worldly things. Perhaps Cuthbert was aware of Wilfrid's growing reputation and wealth. They were both born the same year, and Cuthbert, who was by no means entirely critical of all things Roman, possibly did envy Wilfrid's life from time to time. If this were so, Cuthbert becomes even more of an inspiration to those who are seduced by materialism today.

Aidan's ministry clearly influenced King Oswald and King Oswin, who succeeded Oswald in 642 A.D. Aidan developed a very special friendship with Oswin, whom he loved dearly. It was a mutual love, and one day Oswin expressed this by giving Aidan a very fine horse. He worried about Aidan's health, since Aidan regularly walked long journeys to share the gospel. Not long after this, Aidan met a poor man who begged for alms. In response, Aidan gave him the horse. Soon after, Oswin invited Aidan for dinner and, on the way in, he took Aidan to task for giving away his fine horse. Had he known that Aidan would give it away, he would have given him one of his worst horses, he declared. Aidan at once answered, "What are you saying, your Majesty? Is this child of a mare more valuable to you than this child of God?" With this, they went in to dine.

Aidan sat at the table, but the king stood by the fire rather restlessly. Suddenly he unbuckled his sword, throwing it down, and then knelt at Aidan's feet and begged his forgiveness. Aidan duly forgave him and Oswin sat down and began to converse. But Aidan grew more and more serious until he started to openly weep. All who were present were quite mystified. Then Aidan leaned across to his chaplain who was near him and said, "I know the king will not live very long; for I have never before seen such a humble king. I feel he will soon be taken from us, because this nation is not worthy of such a king."

It was indeed a prophetic word, for a few days later King

Oswin was assassinated. This was the second king loved by Aidan who had died a violent death. Such were the wounds on Aidan's heart that, only eleven days after Oswin's death, Aidan himself was taken from this world, dying at Bamburgh on 31 August 651 A.D. Today, inside St. Aidan's Church at Bamburgh, a place is marked as the one where Aidan began his journey home to paradise.[7]

Fragile Protest Movements

The Celtic commitment to a life of holiness expressed in poverty and simplicity profoundly challenges the consumerist mentality of our day. It also challenges the church's use of power and wealth at every level. In the early witness of Christian life in Britain, there were two expressions of Christian faith: one that was uncritically linked with the values of a collapsing empire, and the other that took Jesus' teaching in the Sermon on the Mount at face value and dared to live it.

We can't go back in time, or pretend that history has not taken place. We have to start from now, and the fact is that we do have large numbers of church buildings, many of them great and grand and finely adorned. We do have church structures that seem anything but simple. We do have our finance committees, and we have our tendency to empire build. Yet it seems to me that the Celtic Church would not attempt to abolish all of this. Cuthbert was actually concerned about bringing the two sides together, and to some extent he was successful. What we need today are communities of people who have Aidan's gentleness and toughness: a gentleness to understand the vulnerable and the poor and a toughness to challenge the church when it is seduced by power.

In J.B. Priestley's *Midsummer Day's Dream*, three visitors find themselves at a large house in the south of England in the mid-1970s. The nuclear holocaust has taken place, and the family who live in this house are among the few survivors. This little family has, through the trauma of nuclear holocaust, been set free from the conspiracy of materialism, political dogmatism, and scientific rationalism that very nearly destroyed their country.

When the three visitors arrive, representing these three destructive strands in our society, they are puzzled and angry at the family's "outdated" lifestyle of simplicity, love for Earth, and enjoyment of spiritual values. But the family does not try manipulative methods to control or persuade the visitors. They are simply themselves, and like those washed up on the island in Shakespeare's *Tempest*, the three visitors slowly become beguiled by the magic of this place. They are like those who awaken from the sleep. By the time they leave, something within them has come to life. The small community had become a vulnerable protest movement, and it was making its mark, albeit with difficulty, on powerful foes.

In the church today, we need many such small and fragile protest movements, led by people who are prepared to swim against the tide. It is my impression that the Spirit of God is calling us to once again consider the Celtic Church as our model of authenticity and simplicity, not so much to put the church right, but rather so that the church can be freed to once again joyfully and confidently live a beatitude lifestyle in our very confused world. In the coming years many who are wearied by the pressures and demands of our restless world will find themselves washed up on such islands, where they can be reminded of another world which in its simplicity is full of abundant life.

Bible Reading
Matthew 5:1–16 The beatitude lifestyle.

Questions for Reflection and Discussion
1. If you are involved in leadership at any level, either in church or at work, spend some time comparing your way of leading with Aidan's.

2. How do you feel about poverty? Reflect on your own lifestyle. Are you satisfied with it? Are there things you want to change? Are your attitudes nearer to those of the beatitudes than to the consumerism of our day?

3. To what extent is your parish or church a fragile protest movement? How can our church community become one that helps people to wake up?

Prayer

Lord, Aidan was humble and lowly; forgive us for being proud.
Lord, have mercy. Lord, have mercy.
Lord, Aidan was patient; forgive us for being impatient.
Christ, have mercy. Christ, have mercy.
Lord, Aidan witnessed with constant love; forgive us for being
inconsistent.
Lord, have mercy. Lord, have mercy.

O God, your gentle apostle Aidan befriended everyone he met.
Grant us the same humble, Spirit-filled zeal, that we may inspire
others to learn your ways, and thus pass on the torch of faith.
Amen.[8]

Notes

1. Bede, *Ecclesiastical History of the English People* (Penguin, 1990), p. 150.

2. Magnus Magnusson, *Lindisfarne, the Cradle Island* (Oriel Press, 1984), p. 58.

3. Eddius Stephanus, "Life of Wilfrid," in *The Age of Bede* (Penguin, 1988), p. 123.

4. Ian Bradley, *The Celtic Way* (DLT, 1993), p. 14.

5. Bede, *Ecclesiastical History*, p. 150.

6. Bede, "Life of Cuthbert," in *The Age of Bede*, p. 54.

7. The story is related in Bede's *Ecclesiastical History*, ch. 14.

8. *An Office for St. Aidan's Day*, St. Aidan Trust.

Chapter 2

The Preeminence of the Bible

Boisil, Prior of the Community at Melrose

On the night that Aidan died at Bamburgh, a young 16-year-old boy called Cuthbert was looking after a flock of sheep on a hillside that overlooked the Northumbrian coast. When the other shepherds had fallen asleep, Cuthbert was in the habit of spending time in prayer. On this particular night, while he was praying, he suddenly saw a light streaming from the sky. It must have been a similar experience to the shepherds of Bethlehem, because he was also given to hear the songs of the angels praising God. As he looked at these angels, he saw the soul of "some holy man" being taken up into heaven. He was to learn later that it was the soul of Aidan. So impressed was the young Cuthbert by this experience that he decided to join the little Christian community at Melrose.

He made for Melrose which is near the present-day border of Scotland and England and which then was in the kingdom of Bernicia. He went to this community because he had heard of Boisil, who was the prior and who had become well known for his particularly holy life, and for his scholarliness. By chance, Boisil was standing by the monastery gate when Cuthbert arrived. Cuthbert dismounted and went into the church to pray. Bede records, "Boisil had an intuition of the high degree of holiness to which the boy he had just seen would rise, and said just this single phrase to the monks with whom he was standing: 'Behold the servant of the Lord.'"

Boisil took no persuading to accept this young lad into the community and we are told that Cuthbert "watched, prayed, worked, and read harder than anyone else." Cuthbert loved his time at Melrose, and grew close to Boisil. However, as was common in those days, there came a time when the monastery was attacked by the plague which "was ravaging the length and breadth of the country." Both Cuthbert and Boisil were afflicted, but while Cuthbert was healed, Boisil was given knowledge that he would die and that he had only a week to live. Boisil decided to spend the last week of his life with Cuthbert, studying the Bible. Boisil chose St. John's gospel, and so, for seven days, the ailing Boisil and the recovered Cuthbert spent time immersed in this much loved gospel. Bede tells us that they "dealt not with the profound arguments but with the simple things of 'the faith which worketh by love.'" As they read it, so Boisil received prophetic insight into Cuthbert's life, and "unfolded all Cuthbert's future during that week," even to the extent of telling Cuthbert that he would become a bishop, news that Cuthbert was very reluctant to receive. After a week Boisil died, no doubt with his mind and heart filled with St. John's account of the resurrection of Jesus.

The bible was greatly loved by the Celtic Church. The historian Leslie Hardinge writes:

> By far the most influential book in the development of the Celtic Church was the Bible. It molded their theology and guided the worship of the early Christians. It suggested rules of conduct and transformed the ancient laws of Irish and Welsh pagans into Christian statutes. It lay at the foundation of the education of children and youth, and sparked the genius of poets and songwriters. It provided inspiration for the scribes of history and hagiography and affected the language of the common people, becoming the dynamic for the production of the most beautiful hand-written books ever made.[1]

Biblical quotations are found everywhere in Celtic Christian writings. Patrick, one of the earliest Celtic saints, wrote two short works, *Confession* and *Letter to Coroticus* which have survived to this day. One scholar has counted in these works 340 quotations from 46 different books of the Bible! A paragraph from his *Confession* illustrates just how steeped he was in the Scriptures. Here Patrick is defending himself against those who said he was too unlearned and simple:

> But if it had been granted to me even as to others, I would not, however, be silent, because of the recompense. And if, perhaps, it appears to some, that I put myself forward in this matter with my ignorance and slower tongue, it is however, written: "Stammering tongues shall learn quickly to speak peace" (Isa. 32:4). How much more ought we to aim at this— we who are the "epistle of Christ"—for salvation even to the

ends of the earth (Acts 13:47), and if not eloquent, yet powerful and very strong, written in your hearts "not with ink," it is testified..."but by the Spirit of the living God" (2 Cor. 3:3). And again the Spirit testifies, "and rusticity was ordained by the Most High" (Ecclus. 7:15).[2]

It does not make easy reading for the modern reader, but such passages reveal Patrick's dependence on the Bible. It is interesting to note that he, in common with much of the church of his time, freely quoted from the book of Ecclesiasticus.

The pre-Christian Celts were not particularly interested in books. In fact this has always been a problem for historians because our knowledge of the Celts has come from non-Celtic books and writings. The Celts preferred to communicate their experiences and knowledge through songs, poems, and art. If they wanted to record words, they did so by memorizing rather than writing and reading. The emerging Christian communities thus somewhat broke with tradition when they developed their love for the Bible, but true to tradition, they learned large parts of it by heart.

The Bible, Theology, and Vision

The Celtic Church developed a love for those books of the Bible that are particularly intuitive, visionary, and imaginative. The psalms, with their love for creation and their emotional content, were especially appealing, for the Celts were a people who were at ease with the earthiness of creation and of their own emotions. Their favorite gospel was that of John, a mystic and adventurer. Traditionally each evangelist was associated with one of the four beasts referred to in Revelation (4:6ff.), who are before the throne of God. Matthew was the beast with the face of a man; Mark was the lion; Luke was the ox (often pictured as a calf); and John was the eagle. The Celts loved all creatures, but they had a special admiration for the eagle, which was believed to be able to fly higher than any other bird, and also had the eyes to see farther. The eagle had the ability to look beyond, to see things that were invisible to others. The eagle could "see and see and perceive." The Celtic Church loved this kind of seeing as the story about Cuthbert and Boisil illustrates. In the final week of Boisil's life, they read the Bible not as an academic study, but as a guide to the meaning of life. The gospel of John was the perfect companion of both the dying, wise old man, and the young man embarking on a new ministry.

In their love for the gospel they dwelt on the "simple things" (always a complimentary word in Celtic terms) to do with faith and love. As they reflected on the simple things, they became open to prophetic insight.

Cuthbert developed such a reputation for his love for the Bible that, not long after his death, Eadfrith, then bishop of Lindisfarne, began work on an exquisite illuminated copy of the four angels which he did in honor of Cuthbert. This book, now 1300 years old, is in the British Library, and it is one of our finest examples of Celtic Christian art. Obviously a labor of love and affection, and it also offers a clear indication of the respect the Celtic Church had for the Bible. It is a spiritual and theological work, and the intricate pictures and borders are delicate tools that help us excavate the truths of the gospels. In fact the more one studies these illuminations, the more one realizes that Eadfrith was doing his theological reflection through them. A close look at his artwork reveals certain tiny imperfections. There are letters and patterns that are left uncolored, or a pattern that disturbs the natural symmetry of the page. Dr. Mark Stibbe writes:

> In achieving such effects, Eadfrith suggested a whole theology through gaps or differences. In pictures which are notable for their order, symmetry, and harmony, Eadfrith left deliberate omissions or made momentary departures from the rest of the picture. This remarkably post-modern strategy could be interpreted as Eadfrith's way of deconstructing the sense of structure that he has so elaborately created. In a sense, that is precisely what it is. Eadfrith's motivation for this idiosyncrasy can only have been that he was not prepared to make a perfect picture. Only God is perfect. People are imperfect. To create what appeared to be a perfect portrayal of divine truths would be nothing short of pride and even blasphemy.[3]

The fact that a bishop was giving so much of his time to

this work says something in itself about the way the Celtic Church valued the Bible. Leslie Hardinge summarizes this:

> The Celtic Church cherished a deep love for the Bible and, from the Epistles of St. Paul, developed their theology. The Psalms were used in worship and were the inspiration of poets and preachers. Without the influences of the views of church fathers, Celtic theologians set about discovering what the Scriptures meant.... Unlike the theologians of Roman Christianity, who appealed more and more to the teachings of Church and councils, Celtic teachers stressed the Bible. The role of the Scriptures in Celtic Christianity was indeed a vital one, so much so that no thorough study of the beliefs and practices of the Christians of Celtic lands is possible without bearing this fact in mind.[4]

Those who consider Celtic Christianity to be New Age need to take note of this strong commitment to Scripture. This church put its anchor deep into the word of God, and was very wary of espousing pagan customs that conflicted with biblical values. Our Bibles today are printed by the millions, with many different versions for us to choose from. We have lost a great deal in the mass reproduction, but thank God most of us are privileged to have easy access to a Bible. In the 1300 years since Eadfrith worked on his Bible, we have seen swings and moods in terms of reading, understanding, and interpreting Scripture. We have known dark times, when the Bible was reserved only for the clergy and academics, and light times, when it was released to people in their own language. The advent of the printing press and the spiritual surge of the Reformation enabled millions to draw afresh from its life. Great preachers like the Wesleys demonstrated its power to change lives. Then, in the age of Enlightenment, the academic world questioned the authority and authenticity of the biblical books and, for much of this century, the main approach of academics to the Bible has been one of suspicion and skepticism. This has polarized Christians, with radical liberals at one end and fundamentalist evangelicals at the other. All this would have mystified the Celtic Church, which knew nothing of either pole. It would have hated the skepticism of the liberals, but would also have been very uncomfortable with the rigidity of the fundamentalists.

Now that we are moving away from a prevailing enlightenment culture into a post-modern age, we have an opportunity to reappraise how we approach the Bible. We have
much to learn from the Celtic Church with its humble love for
the Bible, its placing of Scripture above reason and tradition,
its willingness to learn large parts of it by heart, and its de-
termination to live according to its guidance. We also need to
recall its openness to the intuitive. In this church we find a
healthy balance of Word and Spirit, where evangelical and
charismatic insights are both valued. The story of Cuthbert
and Boisil illustrates this so beautifully, the reading of the
Word which leads naturally on to the use of the gift of prophecy. It was the prophetic insight developed during devotion
to the Word that enabled Boisil to die in peace, and enabled
Cuthbert to move forward in his ministry with such a secure
foundation.

Bible Reading
Acts 17:1–12 Paul teaches from the Scriptures.

Questions for Reflection and Discussion
1. How do you feel about the Bible? How can you foster ways
of loving it in the way that Boisil and Cuthbert did?

2. Have you ever tried learning parts of the Bible by heart?
Try learning, as a starter, the Beatitudes in Matthew 5:3–10.
Once you have learned them, call them to mind and meditate
on them when traveling, walking, etc.

3. Following the example of Boisil and Cuthbert, choose a
passage from St. John's Gospel and open yourself to the Holy
Spirit speaking prophetically to you. It is fairly unusual for
the Spirit to unfold someone's future in the way Cuthbert's
was unfolded, but the principle is that God speaks personally
to us through Scripture. Allow God to speak to you today.

Prayer

A Prayer before reading the Bible:

I open myself to the wisdom of the Word of God.
I open myself to the guiding of the Word of God.
I open myself to the power of the Word of God.

Father, you spoke your Word and the earth was birthed,
Speak new life to me this day.
Jesus, you came to us as the Word of God,
Speak new life to me this day.
Spirit, you awaken me to the Word of God,
Speak new life to me this day.

Father, Son, Spirit,
Welcome me now to the word of life.[5]

Notes

1. L. Hardinge, *The Celtic Church in Britain* (SPCK, 1972), p. 29.

2. C.H.H. Wright, trans., "The Confession of Patrick 11," in *Aristocracy of Soul*, O'Donoghue (DLT, 1987), p. 103.

3. Mark Stibbe, "The Revival of Anglican Theology: Lessons from Celtic Christianity" in *Anglicans for Renewal*, vol. 56 (Spring 1994).

4. L. Hardinge, *The Celtic Church in Britain*, p. 51.

5. General Prayers, St. Aidan Trust.

Chapter 3

The Importance
of Children

Cuthbert, Prior of Melrose, Bishop of Lindisfarne

As a child, Cuthbert loved to play games with his friends. He was strong and very agile and would often boast of his ability to beat older children at sports such as wrestling, running, and jumping. Later in life, he once told the Bishop Trumwine a story from his childhood that changed his life.

It happened when he was about eight years old (642 A.D.): A large crowd of boys were playing games in a field and Cuthbert was among them, thoroughly enjoying himself. Suddenly an infant who was no more than three years old began to severely reprimand him. Cuthbert could not believe his eyes. This little boy stood before Cuthbert, and in front of the astonished crowd of other children, spoke to him as if he were his father. He told Cuthbert that he should not be wasting his time with games when God was preparing him for something far more important. When Cuthbert laughed along with the other boys, the infant threw himself on the ground and sobbed uncontrollably. Cuthbert began to become concerned and tried to cheer him up, but as he did, the infant looked at him and once again told him to give up idle play and prepare himself for the ministry to which God was calling him. The crowd of onlookers was particularly astonished when he referred to Cuthbert as "most holy priest and bishop."

This experience made a great impression on Cuthbert and he clearly believed that the good things of the kingdom of God were not just for adults, but for children as well. Because he had seen prophetic gifts in an infant, he did not doubt that such gifts were available to the very young.

After Boisil's death, Cuthbert became prior of Melrose, but he would often go off on pastoral and evangelistic visits to neighboring areas. Sometimes on these journeys, he would take a young boy with him as a companion. On one such occasion, he and his young companion grew tired and hungry. Cuthbert always liked to use such experiences as opportunities for teaching and discipline, so he asked the boy,

"What are you going to eat today?" The hungry boy replied, "I was just thinking about that myself," and his stomach told him clearly that they couldn't fast for much longer without doing themselves injury. With characteristic directness of speech, Cuthbert encouraged the boy to "have constant faith and hope in the Lord." As he said this he pointed to the sky and showed the boy an eagle flying overhead. He pointed out to the boy that God is more than able to send food by this eagle. They continued their journey and came to a river, and there was the eagle sitting on the bank. "There is the servant I was telling you about," said Cuthbert, looking at the eagle. He sent the boy to go and look at what the eagle had brought, and sure enough, the bird had caught a delicious fresh fish. The boy delightedly brought it back to Cuthbert, only to be reprimanded by Cuthbert for not giving half to the eagle! This story illustrates that leaders like Cuthbert were always eager to teach children about the things of God.[1]

As we have seen, Cuthbert was greatly inspired by Aidan, who also loved and respected children. It was Aidan who welcomed four brothers into his community on Lindisfarne. Cedd, Cynebil, Caelin, and Chad were Anglo-Saxon boys who lived in Northumbria. It was decided that they should go off to school, and the only school in Northumbria at the time was Aidan's community on Lindisfarne, where children were trained for mission and ministry. The school was very small, consisting of only about twelve boys, but was very influential. At the school, and through being part of the family of Aidan's community on Lindisfarne, the boys learned English and Latin. Along with the monks, they learned large parts of the Scriptures by heart, and they watched the skills of those who lovingly illuminated the gospel manuscripts. They became involved in the rhythm of prayer and worship on the island, and they watched courageous missionaries going off across the sands to evangelize the mainland. Like Cuthbert's boy, they were taken out on various evangelistic expeditions and learned the life of faith. As a youth, Chad spent some time in Ireland. We are told by Bede that during this time he and his good friend, Egbert, were "constantly occupied in prayer, fasting, and meditation on the sacred scriptures." All four of the boys became priests, and two of them, Cedd and Chad, became bishops.

Children and Power

From an early age, children had the expectation of encountering God in supernatural ways. Bede recorded for us the story of Aesica, who was a two-year-old living in a convent at Barking. As was common in those days, the community was attacked by a virulent outbreak of the plague. Little Aesica became fatally ill, and just before he died he called out, "Edith, Edith, Edith." This was the name of one of the nuns. No one knew why he was speaking her name because she lived in a different part of the convent from where the boy lay. Sadly, they watched him die, and when, a little later, they went to find Edith, she was also fatally ill and died only a short time after Aesica. The boy had been given prophetic insight about one of the sisters as he was dying.

There is another story of a young boy dying around the same time who received a vision of Peter and Paul coming to visit him. It is interesting to read such stories, because they are not written with the intention of evoking the "ah, how sweet" reaction that we might offer. The stories speak much more about the respect that children were held in. Their visionary experiences were not doubted or dismissed as childish fantasy, and their prophetic gifts were welcomed. The thought that God could only work through the learned and the articulate was abhorrent to the Celtic Church.

Many of the convents, monasteries, and mixed communities must have been filled with the joyful chatter and laughter of children, who were very much part of the community life. Interestingly, the dying child in the story above was offered the "Viaticum of the Body and Blood of Christ,"[2] showing that the Celtic Church did not see it as impossible for children to receive communion, another sign that they were fully accepted as a part of the worshiping community.

The Celtic Church had taken Jesus' teaching about children and the kingdom of God seriously. In the ninth chapter of

Luke's gospel, there are a series of events which have to do with the contrasting values of power between the kingdom of God and of this world. The chapter includes the giving of power and authority to the disciples by Jesus for their mission to the neighborhood; the puzzlement of the powerful King Herod; the miraculous release of power from Jesus that fed 5,000 hungry people; Peter's moment of triumph as he confessed that Jesus is the Messiah; Jesus' teaching about his suffering and the cross; the extraordinary story of the transfiguration on the mountain; and the story of the impotence of the disciples, when, in the valley, they were unable to deliver a young boy of an unclean spirit. By any standard it is a breathtaking series of events, where genuine power and authority are seen again and again, displayed through apparent vulnerability and weakness. It seems that this was too much for some of the disciples, because they started to argue among themselves about who was the greatest. Jesus' answer to this was to take a little child and give him or her the highest possible value by saying, "whoever welcomes this child in my name, welcomes me" (v. 48). In Matthew's gospel we read the words of Jesus, "Unless you change and become like children, you will never enter the kingdom of heaven. Whoever becomes humble, like this child, is the greatest in the kingdom of heaven" (18:4). Jesus gave children the highest possible value for what they were then, not for what they would be one day.

For three and a half years Captain Alan Price of the Church Army worked as the Children's Officer for Anglican Renewal Ministries and it was a great privilege to have him as part of our team. We learned so much from his unswerving conviction that children should be seen as an essential part of the life of the church. He writes, "Children need to be taught not just about the theory but the practice of living in the Spirit. That is where so much of our children's ministry is weak. We teach children the truths of the gospel (the words of Jesus), but do not lead them into doing the deeds of the gospel (the works of Jesus)."[3]

Anyone who has seen Alan working with children cannot

help but be moved at seeing the way he leads children into an appropriate use of the gifts of the Spirit, through which, in all their delightful childishness, they become ministers of grace not only one to another, but to adults as well. It was this attitude that enabled the Celtic Church to accept the fact that children could prophesy, and were a vital and active part of the church's mission.

Bible Reading
Matthew 18:1–5 Children, greatness, and the kingdom.

Questions for Reflection and Discussion
1. Reflect on your own childhood: What kind of awareness of God did you have? How did you pray? How did adults view your faith? If you attended church, what kind of experience was it for you?

2. With these reflections of your own experience in mind, think of children you know now. Do they have faith, and if so, how strong is it? Thinking of Cuthbert's journey with his young friend, can you go for a walk with a child you are close to, making it an adventure of listening to God?

3. What is it like for children in your church? Do they feel they belong in the life of the church? Is yours a church where charismatic gifts are used? Are the children involved in the use of them? Many children love action songs, and they also enjoy action prayers. Can you think of some simple actions to go with prayers you use in your home or church?

Prayer
The Father bending down from heaven,
come cradle the child within you.
Cradle the child within you.

Jesus, the Son born of Mary, whose heart was pierced,
come heal the wounds within you.
Heal the wounds within you.

The Spirit poured out for Sabbath play,
come release new life within you.
Release new life within you.
Release new life within you.[4]

Notes

1. Bede, "Life of Cuthbert," *The Age of Bede,* ch. 12.

2. The word *viaticum* literally means "provision for a journey." Traditionally it was the giving of the Communion to one who was dying.

3. "Children of the Kingdom," *Anglicans for Renewal,* vol. 55: p. 7.

4. General Prayers, St. Aidan Trust.

Chapter 4

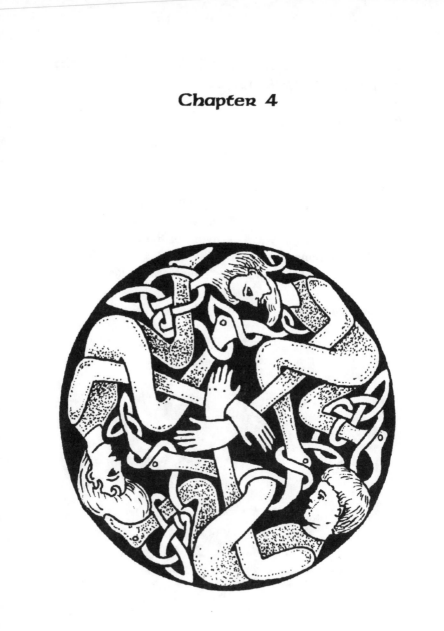

The Celtic Commitment
to Community

Davið, Bishop of Wales

With the departure of the Roman soldiers early in the fifth century and the advance of the Anglo-Saxon invaders into Southern Britain, the Celtic peoples of Britain were pushed west and north. Many retreated to Cornwall and then traveled to the safety of Wales. While it must have been a very disturbing time, it had great benefit for the gospel, because this movement of population enabled the Christian faith to be spread with even greater speed. The Celtic fire was burning bright at Bishop Martin's monastery at Tours; many monks traveled from there across the channel to Cornwall and then on to Wales, establishing the first monastery at Llanbelig in Snowdownia. One such monk was Illtyd, who is regarded by many as the founder of the Christian Church in Wales. He formed his monastic community at Llanilltud Fawr in Glamorgan, which became a great training center.

It was to this training center that the young David came. He was born around 500 A.D. on the westerly tip of Pembrokeshire, which is an area of windswept heathland then known as Menevia. According to legend, his mother, St. Non, gave birth to him during a thunderstorm. He was brought up with the faith, not only learning to read, but also learning the Book of Psalms by heart. He became a monk at Ty Gwyn under the Abbot Paulinus. On one occasion the two went to an island to seek God together in order to find out how God wanted to use them. Paulinus told David that he was being called to gather "bundles of souls" for the kingdom. Inspired by his time at Llanilltyd Fawr and also at Candida Casa (Ninian's community in Scotland), he gathered a mission team and established a total of twelve monastic centers in Somerset, Lincoln, Derby, Hereford, and his native Wales.

In time, David and three close friends spent time praying under the shadow of the Black Mountains and waiting on God for guidance. They were guided by God to build a large and permanent mission center in the valley where David was born, the site of the present St. David's Cathedral. This became a very remarkable community, used as an educational and spiritual center and also to send out countless mission teams to Wales and beyond. David became a bishop in 540 A.D. and died probably in 589 A.D. His final words to the people of Wales were, "Be happy and keep your faith, and do the little things you have heard and seen me do." It was said that after his death kings mourned him as a judge, the older people as a brother, the younger as a father.

It is not surprising that the Celtic Church was so committed to community life. There were three main influences for this.

The first major influence was that of the pre-Christian society. Peter Beresford Ellis writes, "Celtic society displayed a primitive communism, or community-ism, which by the fifth century A.D., when the Brehon Laws of Ireland were first being codified, had developed into a highly sophisticated social system."[1]

The Celtic society readily divided itself into communities of people who had an interest in the needs and rights of individuals, forming primitive "Welfare States." Under Celtic law, the responsibility for providing for the sick or handicapped, a responsibility which was taken very seriously, lay with the tribe. It is believed that Celtic society had six basic social classes, and position was given according to ability and service to the community. As we shall see in Chapter 10, women were more respected in Celtic society than in that of any of its contemporaries, and it was not uncommon for them to rule as chieftains. The Celtic Church inherited a model community that could be very easily Christianized.

The second major influence was that of the Desert Fathers and Mothers, who were a great inspiration to the Celtic Church. As we saw in Chapter 1, this renewal movement was fueled by the compromise and nominalism that was affecting large parts of the church throughout the Roman Empire. Much of the life and witness of the Desert Christians was carried out within the community. It was the beginning of monasticism, and a form of monasticism that the Celtic Church found very attractive. Although the climate and situation of Britain were very different from the hot deserts of Egypt, there were principles—simplicity, prayer, fasting, spiritual warfare, wisdom, and evangelism—that were easy to translate to the communities of these isles.

The third influence was the Celtic Church's love for the Trinity. For them, the Father, Son, and Holy Spirit existed in perfect community, and therefore, the church needed to express this community life while it sought to serve the God, who is Three. Esther de Waal writes, "The prominence given to the Trinity conveys to us something of how these men and women felt about themselves and their world. A God who is Trinity in unity challenges self-centered isolation and points instead to fellowship."[2]

With these influences so deeply within them, the life of the Christian Church inevitably revolved around communities. Ian Bradley writes, "The dominant institution of Celtic Christianity was neither the parish church nor the cathedral, but the monastery, which sometimes began as a solitary hermit's cell and often grew to become a combination of commune, retreat house, mission station, hotel, hospital, school, university, arts center, and power-house for the local community—a source not just of spiritual energy but also of hospitality, learning, and cultural enlightenment."[3]

The Celtic Monastery

These communities were found scattered all over Britain and Ireland. Some of them were tiny communities of only a few huts, but others, like Columba's community on Iona or Brigid's at Kildare, were huge and made quite an impact on the bigger community of the nation. There were both celibate and married monks. Some communities were single sex, others were mixed. It was not uncommon for women to be abbesses of mixed communities, as was the case for Hilda's community at Whitby.

Life in the monasteries varied. Some, following the example of the Desert Fathers, sought out remote and wild places and practiced lives of austerity. Many of the rocks and scattered isles around the shores of these lands were occupied by hermits or small monastic communities. Visitors to Skellig

Michael, the rocky island off the southwest tip of the Kerry coast, can see the ancient beehive cells which have survived centuries of Atlantic gales. Other communities were far less ascetic, although always simple.

The typical monastery would have been a gently busy place in which there was a steady rhythm of work, study, prayer, and mission. Rhigyfarch, the twelfth-century biographer of David, described life in his monastery: "They place the yoke upon their shoulders; they dig the ground tirelessly with mattocks and spades; they carry hoes and saws for cutting and providing with their own efforts for all the needs of the community."

Ray Simpson, Guardian of the Community of Aidan and Hilda, writes of David's community:

> After work in the fields, there was study before they chanted psalms in church and knelt in vigil until twilight. After a simple meal and three more hours of prayer, they slept until cock-crow. They had all things in common, no one should even say "this is my book." Their clothing was basic, mainly skins. David upheld St. Paul's rule: "If a person will not work, he will not eat." Although the brothers had only one proper meal each day, they prepared appetizing meals for the sick and aged guests. The tenth-century Laws of Howell make clear that the monasteries were more a fellowship than a hierarchy. Though the abbot had particular responsibilities, gifts of money had to be shared equally between them all. The large monasteries were divided into households each of which had one priest.[4]

Every monastery, whether large or small, was called a *muinntir*, which means "people." The Celtic monasteries emphasized the human character of their communities and were suspicious of the hierarchical, institutional counterparts in Europe that were far less personal. Each person in these communities was responsible to an *anamchara*, which means "soul friend." The idea of the soul friend came directly from the Desert communities. There, the soul friend was a kind of spiritual guide and counselor, one with whom you could share your own spiritual growth. Soul friends were a very important part of the support structure of the Celtic communities, and there was a well known saying at the time that a person without a soul friend was like a body without a head. Soul friends had no status, they could be clergy or lay. This system dispersed the authority of the community away from one particular person or hierarchical group, to this network of support people.

All bishops were part of a community and would respect the authority of their community. They were bishops of communities of peoples, rather than ruling areas of land. The idea of "ruling a diocese" was quite foreign to the Celtic way of thinking. At the heart of the monastery was worship in the chapel, which was of a simple construction. If they had built with stone, they would have been more inclined to follow the custom of the Eastern Orthodox churches, which were modeled after the simplicity and beauty of a flowering plant rather than a fortress with towers and battlements.

Community and Healing the Land

The Celtic Church flourished at a time when there was a great deal of tribal conflict among the various regional groups that made up the lands that we now call Britain and Ireland. But with the spread of Christianity, the communities became resources for healing the hurts and divisions between the wider communities. The Celtic heart's irrepressible urge to travel meant that there was much coming and going between communities and an eagerness to learn about how other tribes and nations worked and thought.

Pre-Christian Celts were bold warriors and enjoyed conquering land, but the Christianized Celts preferred to work for peace between nations. The Anglo-Saxon invasions sadly destroyed many of their attempts for healing the land. Different parts of the country had their own identities of which they were proud, but sadly, the invasions of the Anglo-Saxons disturbed much of this. For example, the Celtic peoples in the West called themselves Cymru "the land of comrades." (The name Cymru was also used by the Celts in the Northwest, which is how we have the name "Cumbria" today.)

However, the invading Anglo-Saxons renamed this area Wales, which means "the land of foreigners." This was typical of the suspicions, caricatures, and prejudices that developed with the emergence of the separate nations of Wales, England, Scotland, and Ireland. You cannot help but feel that the community that God intended for this group of islands was continuously damaged by the darkness of evil and human sin. Interestingly, many are now looking back to the Celtic Church as a resource for healing the hurts and divisions between the nations.

As we study the Celtic Church, we find an attractive network of Christian communities which speak powerfully to our often individualistic and fragmented church of today. The encouraging thing is to discover that there was a time in the history of this land when genuine *koinonia* "Christian fellowship" existed and flourished and, as we shall see in Chapter 8, this played a key role in evangelism. The Celtic Church was a model of community life that was non-exclusive and deeply attractive to a society that was confused and broken. In this late twentieth century, more than anything else, we need a church after which to model a Spirit-inspired community where people are free to become fully human. The Roman Catholic base communities flourishing among the poor of Latin America have a lot in common with these Celtic communities, and they are one of the most effective evangelistic witnesses that we have today.

If we study the principles of the community life of this ancient church and sensitively adapt them for the communities of today, then not only will we discover true *koinonia* developing in our churches, but we will find that the evangelistic task before us will flow much more freely. We will also find a resource for the healing needed in the community of nations.

Bible Reading
Acts 2:41–47 The fellowship of the early church.

Questions for Reflection and Discussion
1. One of the direct results of the coming of the Holy Spirit to the church at Pentecost was the gift of community. Take some

time to reflect on your church. To what extent is it a community? How does its life compare with that of the early Celtic communities? What can you do to foster a deeper *koinonia* in your church?

2. Do you have an *anamchara*, or soul friend? If not, would you find it useful to have someone whom you could meet with from time to time to share your spiritual journey? Is there someone you could approach who could become your soul friend?[5]

3. What kind of model of community does your church offer to the wider community around you? Does it speak of a radical alternative to the values of individualism and materialism espoused by many today?

Prayer

May the love of Three give birth to a new community.
May the yielding of the Three give birth to a new humanity.
May the life of the Three give birth to a new creativity.
May the togetherness of the Three give birth to a new unity.
May the glory of the Three give birth to a new age.[6]

Notes

1. Peter Beresford Ellis, *Celtic Inheritance* (Constantinople, 1985), p. 16.

2. Esther de Waal, *The Celtic Vision* (DLT, 1988), p. 12.

3. Ian Bradley, *The Celtic Way* (DLT, 1993), p. 70.

4. Ray Simpson, *A Pattern of Worship for St. David's Day*, St. Aidan Trust, 1994.

5. There are a number of books on the subject of soul friends and spiritual direction. Many people have found Kenneth Leech's *Soul Friend* (DLT) very helpful.

6. *A Morning Office in the Celtic Tradition for Trinity Season and Mondays*, St. Aidan Trust, 1994.

Chapter 5

Love of God's Creation

Columba, Dove of the Church

I n the early summer of 521 A.D. in County Donegal, a young lady called Eithne, who was expecting her first child, had a dream. In this dream an angel came to her holding a garment that shimmered with light. He held the dazzling garment in the breeze and it seemed to float over the hills and valleys to a great distance. He said to her, "You will have a son, and his light and influence shall be carried far, far beyond the hills you can see or the world you hear of. He will belong to God and he will bring many souls into the Kingdom of God." On 7 December of that year, Columba was born, and he would indeed travel far and bring many souls into God's Kingdom.

From an early age it was clear that Columba had a special calling, and as a child he was nicknamed Columcille, "Dove of the Church." He was made a Deacon at Moville in County Down in 540 A.D., and then moved to Clonnard in County Meith where Finnian had founded a monastery in 520, which, by the time Columba arrived, numbered about 3000 students. But he was not one for settling, and he was soon on the move again. He traveled north to Ulster, where he established a monastic settlement at Derry in 546 A.D. He always had a special love for Derry, the reason being, he wrote, "for its quietness, for its purity; for it is full of angels white, from one end to another." Such was his love for God's creation, that he made sure the monastery was built without a tree being cut down. In one of his poems, he wrote that he was more afraid of the sound of an axe in Derrywood than he was of hell itself.

The Celtic restlessness was strong in Columba and he spent the next fifteen years establishing churches and monasteries, apparently as many as three hundred. In 560 Columba's life was dramatically changed, he was accused of illegally copying a very precious and beautiful Book of Psalms. Columba was deeply hurt by this incident, not least by the king, who opposed him. His anger burned within him to such an extent that in 561 he got involved in a major battle against the king, a battle which the king lost. It was well known that Columba was behind the opposing forces, and a synod was called in which he was judged. It was clear that Columba had to leave his beloved homeland, which must have hurt him deeply, though his traveling instinct would have made him welcome any adventure. He sought advice from his soul friend, a hermit of Lough Erme, and he was told that he must win as many souls for Christ as had been lost in the battle at Cul Dreimne.

Thus it was that he set off on his famous voyage in 563 with twelve companions. The wind swept his little boat across the sea to the island of Iona, where he formed a monastery that soon became one of the most influential mission centers ever. Today visitors to Iona are still captivated by the light, the colors of the rocks and stones, the wildness of the Atlantic waves and winds, the remoteness, and, perhaps most of all, by a sense of the Spirit of God, who has moved and inspired many generations of Christian people since Columba's arrival. Columba died on Iona on 9 June 597, the same year that Augustine arrived in Canterbury on his Roman mission to convert the English. Our knowledge of Columba comes from his biographer Adomnan, who described Columba as a man "gladdened in his inmost heart by the joy of the Holy Spirit."

Columba was a figure who was greatly loved by the Celtic Church, not least because of his love for creation. This love is beautifully expressed in one of his poems:

> Delightful it is to stand on the peak of a rock, in the
>   bosom of the isle, gazing on the face of the sea.
> I hear the heaving waves chanting a tune to God in heaven; I
>   see their glittering surf.
> I see the golden beaches, their sands sparkling; I hear the joy-
>   ous shrieks of the swooping gulls.
> I hear the waves breaking, crashing on rocks, like
>   thunder in heaven. I see the mighty whales.
> I watch the ebb and flow of the ocean tide; it holds my secret,
>   my mournful flight from Ein:
>
> Contrition fills my heart as I hear the sea; it chants my sins,
>   sins too numerous to confess.
> Let me bless almighty God, whose power extends over sea and
>   land, whose angels watch over all.
> Let me study sacred books to calm my soul; I pray for peace,

kneeling at heaven's gates.
Let me do my daily work, gathering seaweed, catching fish,
giving to the poor.
Let me say my daily prayers, sometimes chanting, sometimes
quiet, always thanking God.
Delightful it is to live on a peaceful isle, in a quiet cell, serving
the King of Kings.[1]

This is a beautiful example of the Celtic Church's ability to experience God through God's creations. Columba started by standing on a rock gazing out to sea. As he heard the sound of the sea, it became for him a heavenly tune. The waves spoke to him of the thunder of heaven. As he watched the tide ebb and flow, it spoke to him of comings and goings, and it caused him to reflect on his departure from Ireland. Then he was remorseful and repentant as he thought about Cul Dreimne, but he was not condemnatory. No, God had forgiven him and therefore he could bless the Lord, whose power extends over sea and land. He reflected further on what he saw, and he thought about his daily work of studying, gathering food, and feeding the poor. Finally, he was moved to think about prayer, which, like the sea, is sometimes still and quiet and is, at other times, filled with song.

The poem is a hymn of praise which was aroused in Columba as he stood on his rock and listened to God's good creation. There is no pantheism here, but a true and godly appreciation of nature, an appreciation that is seen in many of the psalms which Columba would have learned by heart. The Celts loved the psalms for many reasons, one of which was their love for creation. The poem above is full of the imagery of Psalm 29:

The voice of the Lord is over the waters;
the God of glory thunders,
the Lord over mighty waters.
The voice of the Lord is powerful;
the voice of the Lord is full of majesty.

Such biblical passages appealed very much to the Celts because of their previous druid-led pagan religion, which also had a very high regard for nature. Ian Finlay writes, "The Celtic

Church grew among people who were not builders, who were not tempted to follow a tradition of containing their gods in temples, but felt closer to them where they could feel the wind buffeting their faces, and see the flash of white wings against the sky, and smell the sun-warmed bark of trees."[2]

The Christian community saw nothing wrong in this respect for nature and they found it very easy to incorporate it into their Christian life and witness. In fact, their Christian faith actually enhanced their love for creation. Many Celtic communities were formed in wild and remote places, for it was here that they could feel the power of the wind and the strength of the sea. Anyone who has been to Lindisfarne or Iona during bad weather knows all about this. The first time I visited Lindisfarne the rain fell continuously and most of the time horizontally, carried by the northeasterly gale. I remember walking around the coast of the island in these conditions, getting soaked and buffeted, and feeling so aware of the power and glory of God. In our Western society, where we do all we can to protect ourselves from cold, wind, and wet, we miss this closeness to creation that the early Celtic communities experienced. This need for protection has been partly to blame for our lack of concern for creation and ecological issues. It also contributes to our lack of a sense of adventure. David Adam, in his book *Borderlands*, speaks about the need for us to experience the borderlands:

> Today we are very much in danger of producing "midlander" mentality and emotions: those of safe people who have never been all at sea or experienced the "cliffs of fall" (as the poet Gerard Hopkins described the mind's mountains of grief). We avoid being frontiersmen and women in case we are shot at by our own side if we dare to cross boundaries. Yet in reality, life is ever taking us to the edge of things. Borders may be hard to see or define, but we forever cross into new lands. Frontiers are still exciting places and everyone should be encouraged to explore them: The borderlands are there for us all to enjoy.[3]

If we have never spent time in natural borderlands, such as where the land meets the ocean or where day becomes night, then we will find the borderlands of human experience harder to face and understand.

God's Presence in Creation

Jesus frequently referred to nature when he wanted to teach an important spiritual truth. He spent a lot of time teaching the disciples how to understand the many messages in creation. Noel O'Donoghue has written a book called *The Mountain Behind the Mountain*. The title is based on a phrase taken from a poem by Kathleen Raine called "The Wilderness." A stanza from this poem reads:

> Yet I have glimpsed the bright mountain behind the mountain,
> Knowledge under the leaves, tasted the bitter berries red,
> Drunk cold water and clear from an inexhaustible hidden fountain.

O'Donoghue explains the Celtic understanding of this phrase, "the mountain behind the mountain":

> The mountain of that kind of Celtic tradition to which Kathleen Raine belongs, and which nurtured the people from which I came, is neither an ideal nor a mythical mountain, nor is it exactly a holy or sacred mountain in the sense of a mountain made sacred by theophany or transfiguration. No, it is very ordinary, very physical, very material mountain, a place of sheep and kine, of peat, and of streams that one might fish in or bathe in on a summer's day. It is an elemental mountain, of earth and air and water and fire, of sun and moon and wind and rain. What makes it special for me and for the people from which I come is that it is a place of Presence and a place of presences. Only those who can perceive this in its ordinariness can encounter the mountain behind the mountain.[4]

The Celtic Church was always on the lookout for signs of God's presence in God's creations. David Adam writes of how the Celtic Church sought to develop the eye of the eagle, a creature they much admired: "They prayed that their eyes might be opened, that all their senses might be made alert to that which was invisible. They prayed that they might have the eagle's eye to see Him who comes at all times....They soared to the heights of awareness and saw deeper than many peoples, for they sought to see with the eye of the eagle."[5]

The Celts therefore carried an expectation of meeting God in God's creation and were constantly on the lookout for something new to learn through the multitude of parables available to them. They were aware of God's presence, and of the presence of angels. References to angels are frequent in the stories of the Celtic saints, who treated them as a very normal part of God's creation. There are also many references to demons, as well as to those who have died in faith, who are also part of this created order. Places where people died and where their bones were laid in the earth were very important to the Celtic Church. The burial place was a reminder of the company of witnesses who pray for us and encourage us (Hebrews 12:1).

Care for Creation

The Celtic love for creation also included the animal world. Just as Jesus was in the wilderness with wild beasts who were not hostile to him, the Celtic Church recognized that people giving themselves to prayer could be less fearful of the animal kingdom. There are not only many stories of Celtic saints showing love and concern for animals and birds, but also many stories of animals and birds showing concern for the saints.

Cuthbert seems to have had a special affection for the animal kingdom. There is a famous story of Cuthbert, when he was prior at Melrose, being invited by Abbess Aebbe to spend a few days at the mixed convent at Coldingham. It was apparently his habit to go into the sea up to his shoulders at night and pray for hours in the cold waters. This in itself tells us something about the effect of prayer in relation to creation. It is not uncommon to find examples of people praying and worshiping God in cold places and finding themselves filled with warmth, as if the previous hostility of the cold has been subdued. At the end of this night vigil in the water, Cuthbert came to shore where two otters bounded out of the water and warmed his feet with their breath and tried to dry him on their fur.

Later in his life, when he was on Farne Island, there is the story of Cuthbert speaking sternly to the crows who were eating all the seeds he was sowing. "Why are you eating crops you yourselves did not grow?" he asked them indignantly.

"Perhaps you have greater need of them than I. If God has given you permission, then do as He bade you; if not, be off with you and stop damaging other people's property!" Apparently they duly obeyed. Bede informs us that Cuthbert was inspired by the Desert Father, Anthony, who spoke severely to a donkey that was threatening to trample down his little garden.[6]

Columbanus was said to be very fond of a number of wild beasts who would come and play with him. On one occasion twelve wolves came up to him while he was saying a psalm. They were so taken with Columbanus and the psalm, that they meekly stood by him before going away. There are also stories of him talking to the squirrels. Such stories of Cuthbert and Columbanus should not be seen simply as quaint, they carry a much deeper significance. It is not at all unlikely that the very strong presence of the Spirit of God in such people affected the animals' response to them.

In Romans 8:19–24, Paul tells us of the eager yearning in creation to be freed from its bondage to decay, and its waiting for the revealing of the children of God. According to this passage, the Spirit has a key role in this releasing. It was the expectation of the Celtic Church that the outpouring of the Spirit of God's people would influence creation. This theme was taken up by Francis, whose love for creation was very much at the heart of his spirituality. It is interesting to note that Columbanus established a community at Bobbio in Italy, to which the young Francis came in later years. He was greatly impressed by this Celtic community, and it was there that he developed his love for creation. Therefore, there is a historical connection at Bobbio between Celtic and Franciscan spirituality.

We have then, in Celtic Christian spirituality, a thoroughly creation-affirming spirituality. But their fixation on creation was not at the cost of redemption. Because they were so attuned to creation, they became very aware of creation's signals about the need for the redeeming work of Christ. A Celtic saint who illustrates this well is Chad, who formed a monastic community at Lichfield. Bede tells us that "if a gale rose while he was reading or doing anything else he would at once call upon God for mercy and pray him to show mercy on mankind." The stronger the storm, the more earnest was Chad's praying. When his monks asked Chad why he did this, he replied, "have you not read, 'The Lord thundered in the heavens, and the Highest gave his voice?'" He was quick to point out that the purpose of the thunder and lightning was to remind people of the judgment to come, and our response should be to "examine our inmost hearts, purging the vileness of our sins."[7]

The Celtic Church was all too aware of the damage done to creation by human sin and Satan's rebellion, and so they had a great love for the cross. You can still see today in Ireland many examples of the huge standing crosses, planted firmly in the soil as a sign of Christ's redeeming work in the heart of God's good, but damaged, creation. In the words of Euros Bowen, a modern Welsh poet, "*Nid oes atgyfodiad lle nad oes pridd*" (There is no resurrection where there is no earth).[8]

As we shall see in Chapter 13, the Celtic Church was also very aware of evil influences in creation, which meant that they would not have been tolerant of some New Age approaches to creation, which make no allowance for the fact that matter can be infected with dark and demonic forces.

But the tendency in the Western Church has been to be too negative about creation. Sadly, the church has been far too interested in spiritual things, and has not shown sufficient care for the earth on which we live. It is sad and shameful that non-Christian groups like Greenpeace and Friends of the Earth have been at the forefront of loving our planet. Thank God there have been people who have taken up this challenge, but how much better if the lead had been taken by Christian people with a biblical view of creation.

Noel O'Donoghue talks about the "priestly" role of the church in bringing together the divine and human world. God has ordained it that the Christian community has been empowered to have a great influence for good on this earth. We have been entrusted with the work of blessing our land. But if we fail to do this, there are principalities and powers of darkness that are all too ready to contaminate the earth. Our failure to take this priestly duty seriously has allowed much darkness to spread in our lands. Old customs like beating the bounds and rogation days developed from a spirituality that saw the sense in blessing the ground. Today we are seeing such customs being restored as spiritually effective rituals which bless the earth. I am sure we shall see other rituals developing as we take this priestly role more seriously.

Bible Reading
Genesis 1:1–2:3 God made the good earth.

Questions for Reflection and Discussion
1. What are your feelings about creation? Have you heard God through God's creation? What can you do to become more aware of God speaking to you in this way?

2. Have you been in a natural "borderland?" How did it feel? Why not plan to go for a walk in the rain!

3. Is there any way in which you can show your concern for creation? How can you fulfill your "priestly" duty to the creation around your home? Is there land around you which needs healing either because it is physically polluted by chemicals or waste, or because it is spiritually polluted by a history of battles, human sin, or injustices? Is there any action you or your church could do to bring healing to the land?

Prayer
A Midday Prayer

As the press of work ceases at noon,
May God's rest be upon us.

As the sun rides high at noon,
May the sun of righteousness shine upon us.

As the rain refreshes the stained, stale land,
May the Spirit bring rain upon our dry ground.[9]

Notes

1. Quoted in Robert Van de Weyer's *Celtic Fire* (DLT, 1990), p. 33, 34.

  2. Ian Finlay, *Columba*, p. 107.

  3. David Adam, *Borderlands* (SPCK, 1991), p. viii.

  4. Noel O'Donoghue, *The Mountain Behind the Mountain* (T&T Clark, 1993), p. 30.

  5. David Adam, *Eye of the Eagle* (Triangle, 1990), p. 11.

  6. *The Age of Bede*, p. 68, 69.

  7. Bede, *Ecclesiastical History*, IV.3.

  8. Euros Bowen, *Gwreiddyn Tàp (Tap Root)* (Church in Wales Publications, 1993), p. 132f.

  9. *Midday Office*, St. Aidan Trust.

Chapter 6

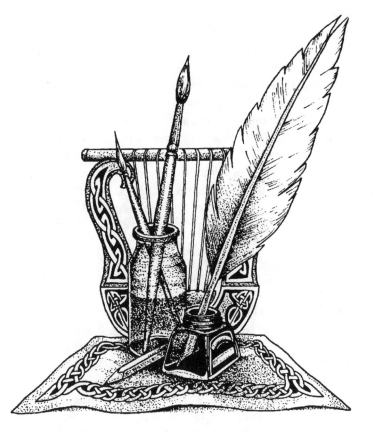

The God-Given Gift
of Creativity

Hilда, Abbess of Whitby, and Caeдmon

From its small beginnings on the island of Lindisfarne, the Celtic Church in Northumbria grew quickly, spreading out in a network of community bases. Many of these centers became large and thriving monasteries. One such monastery was at a place called Straenaeshalch, known more commonly as Whitby. This was a mixed community and the first abbess was Hilda, whom Aidan greatly respected and appreciated. Although of royal heritage, Hilda had a great love for all people, and was committed to seeing a new community form at Whitby in which social distinctions had no meaning.

Into this community came a man called Caedmon who had "followed a secular occupation until well advanced in years." When he came to this community, Caedmon knew nothing about poetry. In Celtic communities, when there was a feast, it was a well established custom that all the guests would in turn be invited to sing and entertain the others. Caedmon had a reputation for leaving the gathering just as the harp was about to be passed to him.

On one such occasion, he left the party just in time to avoid having to sing and play. That night it was his duty to look after the community animals, and he settled down in the stable to sleep. He then had a powerful dream that changed his life. He dreamed that he saw a man who came and stood beside him and called his name. This man looked hard at him and then said, "Caedmon, sing me a song." Caedmon was appalled—he knew he could not sing. But this time there was no slipping out of the party. "I can't sing," confessed the very worried Caedmon. The man continued to look at him, and then calmly said, "But you shall sing to me." And this visitor asked him to sing about no less a subject than the creation of all things. Suddenly Caedmon found himself singing of the most profound things about God in beautiful melody. We have a record of the opening of this song from Bede:

Praise we the fashioner now of Heaven's fabric,
The majesty of his might and his mind's wisdom,
Work of the world-warden, worker of all wonders,

How he the Lord of Glory everlasting,
Wrought first for the race of men Heaven as a rooftree,
Then made he Middle Earth to be their mansion.[1]

Bede tells us that this is the general sense of the words, which are translated from the original language.

Caedmon awoke in the morning filled with amazement about the dream. He went to see Hilda to tell her about his experience. She invited Caedmon to give an account of his dream before a number of learned people, so they could assess the quality and origin of the gift. All agreed that this was a gift given by God. Caedmon was immediately welcomed formally into the community, and he was taught about doctrine and history. As he learned about these things, his task was to turn them into poems and songs.

And so Caedmon spent the rest of his life in this community, composing songs and poems on all the major stories and events from the Bible. His works ranged from his first song of creation that he sang in the dream, to sobering poems on the last judgment, to joyful songs about heaven. Just before he died, Caedmon had a strong sense that he was living his last days. On the evening of his death, he asked to receive communion, and then, Bede records, "his tongue, which had sung so many inspiring verses in praise of his Maker, uttered its last words in his praise as he signed himself with the Cross, and commended his soul into his hands." Thus died one of the greatest Celtic poets.

It was not difficult for the Celtic Church to accept the existence of this kind of creative gift into their community; in Celtic society, the bard was a very significant figure. Peter Beresford Ellis identifies for us six basic social classes in Celtic society. The lowest social class was the "non-freemen." The Celts were opposed to slavery, so this group was not so much slaves as lawbreakers. The next group was the people who owned land and hired themselves out for labor. The next was made up of those who owned land and worked it. The fourth class was sometimes described as the "Celtic nobility," which is a rather misleading title: They were more of a civil service class. The fifth class was the professional class and in this group were the druids, lawyers, doctors, and, most significantly, the bards, the poets, the storytellers, and the minstrels. These were a well trained body of people who were highly regarded in Celtic society. Peter Beresford Ellis writes of this group:

> They were a well trained body of men and women who were highly regarded in society. The Celts were avid in their pursuit of knowledge, of literacy, and learning. This group were the repositories of Celtic folklore, legends, history, and poetry. They usually held a salaried position in the retinue of a chieftain. Training a bard was almost as lengthy as training a druid. Diodorus Siculus, Posidonius, and Athenaeus have all noted the popularity of music among the Celtic peoples and mention a wide variety of instruments in use including lyres, drums, pipes, trumpets, and a harp-like instrument.[2]

As the Celtic peoples were converted to Christ, it must have been a great delight to them to find a faith that was so filled with creative life, a faith that affirmed their inherent delight of music, poetry, and art. As we shall see in Chapter 12, the Celtic Church preferred to communicate in ways that made full use of the God-given gift of imagination. Poetry, storytelling, music, and art were all excellent vehicles for teaching profound truths in ways that not only fed the mind, but enlightened the spirit and warmed the heart. It was therefore not at all surprising to find that people like Caedmon had a great influence in the community. The only unusual thing in the story of Caedmon is his sudden discovery of these gifts. He became the community bard overnight, whereas in pre-Christian Celtic society, he would have required years of training. Such is the disturbance of charismatic gifts!

Gaelíc Songs and Poems

Anyone who visits Cornwall, Wales, Ireland, or Scotland, and spends time with the people and customs, will soon find they are among a people who have a rich vein of poetry and storytelling deep in their souls, and in their history. In 1832, a man called Alexander Carmichael was born on the island of Lismore, off the coast of Argyll. He grew up listening to fami-

ly tales of an ancestral connection with the church of
Columba, and he fell in love with this Gaelic church and its
missionaries. Following his education, he found work with
Customs and Excise. His duties necessitated making regular
journeys to the Highlands and Islands, where the English language was virtually unknown. Like an excited archaeologist,
he started to discover songs, hymns, chants, and poems that
were centuries old and had been beautifully preserved in the
Gaelic culture. He discovered such abundance of this rich resource, that he started to compile a written collection, largely
between 1855 to 1899. The more he traveled to these isles, the
more enchanted he became with the prayers, songs, and
poems. At his own expense he went on many "collecting pil-
grimages," often tramping along peaty paths in high winds
and rain to find a remote crofter's cottage, where he would
stop and collect a further prayer or hymn to meticulously
write down for his collection.

Carmichael's collection eventually reached six volumes, the
first of which was published in 1900. The Gaelic title for the
work is *Ortha nan Gaidheal*. The English collection has been
given a Latin title *Carmina Gadelica* (Gaelic songs) and is currently published in one volume.[3] In this collection there is a
whole host of hymns and prayers, some of which will feel
strange to English Protestants.[4] Noel O'Donoghue writes of
the *Carmina Gadelica*, "The contents of these volumes, hymns,
and prayers, dating for the most part to the sixteenth century,
are unique in Christendom in the beauty of language, in the
freshness of imagery, and in the depth and immediacy of the
piety expressed in a kind of domestic liturgy centered around
the homestead and the little world of island crofting communities."[5]

In this collection, the Celtic love for poetry is apparent. It
has much to teach our twentieth-century world, which has
given itself so much to prose inspired by the rationalism of
the enlightenment era. Yet there are clear signs that we are
emerging from this particular dark age, and there is no doubt
that in the coming years the church will need to rediscover the
ministry of the Christian bard. Stewart Henderson, a modern-

day Christian poet who is acutely aware of the need for the church to recapture its lost poetry, writes:

> Thankfully over the past years there has been a realization within some deep-hearted priests that if you banish poetry and the other expressive arts to the dim cloisters of our faith, then what takes place is in effect the banning of God thinking aloud. But there are still many who view poetry as something of which to be suspicious and to slander as irrelevant. And it is at this point that the English Church, like the country outside its doors, seems to have lost its sight. Not hearing or seeing the full foaming God of the Sea and the Sacraments.[5]

The Visual Arts

This same suspicion is carried over into the world of art. We live in an increasingly visual age, and yet the church is still bound in its addiction to words. As a visitor to many churches, I quite often feel overwhelmed with the amount of words I have to receive, whether they be expressed in the form of a multitude of hymnbooks and service books, or whether they come from the mouths of the worship leaders and preachers. Increasingly, I find myself longing for the visual; and the only places I find myself being given something worth resting my gaze on are either the more ornate Catholic churches, or some of the very exciting new youth services that are developing, through which people are discovering the importance of the visual arts in communication.

The Celtic Church had a deep love for art, and this can be seen most clearly in some of the illustrated manuscripts that have survived to this day. A number of these are very well known, in particular the *Lindisfarne Gospels*, written in Northumbria at the end of the seventh century, the eighth-century *Lichfield Gospel of St. Chad*, and the *Book of Kells* in Ireland, which probably has origins in the eighth century. Anyone looking at these works will be stunned by the intricate design, the bright colors, and the profusion of symbols. Enormous amounts of time and devotion were spent on these paintings.

As with Eastern iconography, only those who were considered to be sufficiently holy were permitted to paint in this way. Thus the painters of the *Lindisfarne Gospels* were a team of two bishops, an anchorite, and a priest. It is quite sobering to contrast the ministry of the bishops of today's church with that of their counterparts in Celtic times. Today's bishop has to face a mountain of administrative paperwork (little of which is artistically attractive), whereas Bishop Eadfrith of Lindisfarne spent hours with quills and brushes, slowly copying the gospels and adding beautiful illuminations. It was a contemplative exercise which no doubt deeply enriched his ministry.

The other expression of early Celtic Christian art that survives today are the engraved pictures and designs on the high standing crosses. Many of these are covered with pictures of stories from the Bible. Standing high and proud by roadsides and on hilltops, these acted like lively evangelistic tracts for the illiterate who could come and read for themselves the good news depicted so beautifully into the stone.

Music

When it comes to the music of the early Celtic Church, we have fewer sources to go on. Alexander Carmichael tells of the music he encountered in his travels into the Hebrides: "The music of the hymns had a distinct individuality, in some respects resembling and in many respects differing from the old Gregorian chants of the Church. I greatly regret that I was not able to record this peculiar and beautiful music, probably the music of the old Celtic Church."[7]

According to Ian Bradley this Celtic plainchant had a more "lyrical, mystical, sinuous quality than the cooler and more controlled Gregorian chant favored by Rome."[8] He goes on to point out that the Celtic Church's music was also very influenced by the sounds of creation. It was quite customary, for example, for people to stand on the seashore and sing music inspired by the sound of the waves. It is interesting to find nowadays a number of music tapes emerging in which the music is influenced by sounds of nature—running water or the sounds of creatures such as whales or seagulls. Ian

Bradley comments on this: "This kind of mouth music, so deeply in tune with the rhythms of nature, is very different from the four-square hymns we have been used to singing in Western churches since the Reformation. But it is perhaps not so different from the Taizé chants, folk-songs, and rhythmic choruses from Africa and Asia which are increasingly coming to enliven our worship and broaden our experience of religious music."[9]

It is my conviction that it is a matter of some urgency that if we want what we do in church to make any sense to those beyond it, we must rediscover these kind of songs of worship. We are living at a time when here is a resurgence of interest in Gregorian chant. Our heavy hymns or disposable choruses just do not make sufficient connections with the deep searchings in the lives of so many.

I find it most exciting that Bradley mentions Taizé and African music. I believe these are two styles of musical worship that we urgently need to listen to if we are to connect with the non-church community, which has little knowledge of church culture. It is interesting to observe that evangelistically, the most effective musical worship is probably that of Taizé, where every summer thousands of non-Christian people flock to the *Eglise de la Reconciliation*. They settle in the stillness of that vast chapel and encounter spiritual depth through music, much of which is in a language they do not understand—so much for our desperate need to find words that make sense to a modern generation! The other experience of sung worship that culturally connects is the music of the black church in Africa. Anyone who has stood in a congregation of black worshipers when they are singing their songs and hymns in their own language, will know that extraordinary experience of being touched, at the very deep place of both our humanity and spirituality, by the rich harmonies.

There is a task before us, therefore, to rediscover Celtic expressions of worship that are in harmony with those who first worshiped the Lord in these lands. Because they were a listening and profoundly mission-minded people, they developed a style of musical worship that worked beautifully. Those who found salvation in Christ through the witness of the church, also discovered a way of singing to him that required no abrupt cultural shift.

Alexander Carmichael was greatly stirred by the music of the Gaelic people that arose from their holistic way of life. We would do well today to listen again to Carmichael: "Perhaps no people had a fuller ritual of song and story, of secular rite and religious ceremony, than the Highlanders. Mirth and music, song and dance, tale and poem, pervaded their lives, as electricity pervades the air."[10]

Bible Reading

Exodus 35:20–35 God inspires Bezalel and Oholiab with artistic gifts.

Questions for Reflection and Discussion

1. When did you last spend time with a poem? If you have a book of poetry nearby, find one that you like and read it carefully. Note how it communicates to you. Why is it that it communicates to your heart as well as your mind? Perhaps you would like to write a poem yourself—why not start now!

2. Spend a bit of time thinking about the Celtic love of art. How much visual communication is there in your church? Can you think of ways that would bring more life, visually, to your church building?

3. Think about the style of music that you have in church. How does it relate to people outside the church? Is there a big cultural leap that people have to make to come into your church? How about going out one day to the sea or a river and praising the Lord in music inspired by his creation!

Prayer

Lord, you are my island; in your bosom I rest.
You are the calm of the sea; in that peace I stay.
You are the deep waves of the shining ocean.
With their eternal sound I sing.
You are the song of the birds; in that tune is my joy.

You are the smooth white strand of the shore; in You is no gloom.
You are the breaking of the waves on the rock; Your praise is echoed
in the swell.
You are the Lord of my life; in You I live.[11]

Notes

1. Bede, *Ecclesiastical History*, p. 248f.

2. Peter Beresford Ellis, *Celtic Inheritance*, p. 19.

3. Alexander Carmichael, *Carmina Gadelica* (Floris Books, 1992).

4. Some people reading the *Carmina Gadelica* will struggle with such terms as "incantations" and "charms," and will be fairly suspicious about talk of fairies! In my view some of the poems and chants do seem fairly superstitious and a few appear occultic. But it is absolutely essential that we don't apply rationalistic evangelical presuppositions to our study of these writings. We will need to approach these writings with a humble sense of exploration, rather than with a censor's pen.

5. Noel O'Donoghue, *The Mountain Behind the Mountain*, p. 41.

6. Stewart Henderson, "If Albion Could Sing Again," *Anglicans for Renewal*, vol. 58, p. 12.

7. Alexander Carmichael, *Carmina Gadelica*, p. 29.

8. Ian Bradley, *The Celtic Way*, p. 91.

9. Ian Bradley, *The Celtic Way*, p. 92.

10. Alexander Carmichael, *Carmina Gadelica*, p. 29.

11. Echoes a prayer attributed to Columba in Mary Calvert's *God to Enfold Me* (Grail, 1993), p. 121f. It is used by St. Aidan Trust in the *Evening Office*.

Chapter 7

Death and the Dead

Drythelm's Triumph over Death

Drythelm was a devout man who lived in Cunningham, Northumbria. The Venerable Bede tells us of a remarkable event that happened to him in his home: Drythelm had started to sicken, probably suffering from one of the many plagues that afflicted communities at that time. One evening his sickness worsened, and his family gathered around him praying for him and willing him to live. However, in the small hours of the night he died, much to the distress of his devoted family. The family remained around his lifeless body, mourning for him. Suddenly, at daybreak, he sat up which terrified everyone gathered around the bed, and all, except his wife, ran out of the room in panic. Trembling with fear she looked at him, and he turned to her and said, "Do not be frightened; for I have truly risen from the grasp of death, and I am allowed to live among people again." He then related to her and many others his after-death experience.

Drythelm said that after he died a handsome man in a shining robe came beside him and led him in what he took to be a northeasterly direction. After a while they came to a very broad and deep valley which stretched for as far as his eye could see. What he saw there was truly horrible: One side of this valley was bitterly cold with snow and hail, and the other was intensely hot with great flames. Both sides were filled with souls of people who had died, and who spent their time desperately going from side to side in a tormented state. Drythelm took this to be hell, but his angel guide, reading his thoughts, said, "This is not hell, as you imagine." He led Drythelm on to a place of dense darkness which he described as a "nocturnal and solitary gloom." Every now and then this gloom was interrupted by a flame shooting up from a great pit. To Drythelm's horror, the angel suddenly left him. Terrified, Drythelm watched these spurts of flame, and as he looked more intensely at them, he saw within them the souls of people being flung in the air, then falling back into the pit. He then heard the sound of "a most hideous and desperate lamentation, accompanied by harsh laughter." Drythelm looked to where this noise was coming from and he saw evil spirits dragging five human souls to the pit. As he watched this, a group of these spirits started to come and torment him, though they did not dare to touch him. He desperately looked for help but found none, until his angel guide appeared again, putting to flight the tormenting demons.

They then continued the journey out from the darkness until they came to an enormous wall, the height and length of which stretched for as far as the eye could see. Suddenly they found themselves on top of this wall, and on the other side Drythelm saw a scene of great bliss. He saw a meadow filled with sweet fragrance and a quality of light he had never seen in his life, and in this meadow, he saw the souls of deeply contented people. He then began to wonder whether this was heaven, but again the angel corrected him and said that this was not heaven and led him on. They came to a place which Drythelm found impossible to describe, but it was a place which made the former meadow pale by comparison. He longed to enter this place, but the angel would not let him and led him back the way they came.

On the return journey he explained to Drythelm what they had seen. The place of the terrible valley of heat and cold had been a kind of purgatory for those who had come to faith right at the end of their lives. They were apparently helped by the prayers of the living, and their ultimate destination was heaven. The fiery pit was the mouth of hell. The fragrant meadow over the wall was for those who had lived good and faithful lives, and were waiting to enter into heaven. According to the angel, those who have lived very saintly lives bypass this stage and go straight to heaven.

Having explained all of this, the angel told Drythelm that he must return to his body and live in this world again. And so it was that he found himself back in his bed, terrifying the group of mourners by sitting up alive and well again. Drythelm told quite a number of people about his experience, including King Aldfrid, Ethelwald, who later became Bishop of Lindisfarne, and a monk called Haemgils, who told the story to Bede. After this experience, Drythelm entered the monastery at Melrose and developed a reputation as one who could talk with great conviction about the reality of heaven and hell, and many came to faith as a result of hearing his remarkable testimony.

In recent years there has been a great deal of near-death or after-death experiences, and much has been written on the subject.[1] When I was a hospital chaplain, I came across two people who had experienced life after death, having been clinically dead for a few minutes on the operating table. Both men were quite overwhelmed by the experience and were unable to tell me about it without weeping.

The notion of people being brought back to life is not difficult for Christians to comprehend. In the pages of the New Testament there are stories of Lazarus, Jairus' daughter, and Tabitha, all of whom were called back to this world from death. We have no account from them of what they experienced in their hours of death, but it is almost certain that they had an interesting story to tell.

The Celtic Church had a much clearer view of this subject than the rather muddled and vague ideas of today's church. Untimely death was much more common due to the ravages of plague and warfare. The arrival of the church with the good news of the resurrection of Jesus from the dead was gladly received by the Celtic communities, though they had by no means a pessimistic view of death. In fact, the druid-led religion of the Celts was one of the first to evolve a doctrine of immortality. They had a two-world view: When you died, your soul passed from this world to the next, which was a much better version of this world. It was also possible for souls to pass from the other world to this world. Newborn babes would carry the souls of those who had previously been in the other world. The church, therefore, did not have to convince people of the existence of the afterlife, but they did have to provide clear teaching about salvation in Christ, the once and for all nature of death, and the reality of heaven and hell.

The Ministry of the Dead

In many ways the Celts were much more at ease with their understanding of death and the dead than modern-day Protestants. Despite the imagery of the huge wall of Drythelm's vision, the Celtic Church believed that the faithful in heaven were free to pray for the church in this world, and on occasion, to visit with an urgent message, usually in a dream or vision. David Adam writes: "For the Celtic Church it was a very thin line that divides the saints triumphant from us on earth. Those who witnessed before us and are received up into glory are very much alive. They are not men and women of the past, but sons and daughters of God, who are alive now and in the fullness of eternal life. The Communion of Saints is a reality to be experienced."[2]

The Celtic Church assumed that those who were particularly good at praying on earth, would carry on this ministry in heaven. Thus we have the story of a young boy at the monastery of Bardney Abbey in Lincolnshire, where the bones of King Oswald were buried. As we have seen, Oswald was the much loved king who was responsible for inviting Aidan to come and convert the English; and it was the custom of the members of that community to go to Oswald's tomb to spend time in prayer. One day a little boy in the community became seriously ill and no medical help could cure him. One of the brothers carried him to Oswald's tomb and laid him there. After spending some time there, the fever passed and the boy recovered and was never afflicted again by this disease. Bede, who narrates the story tells us, "It need cause no surprise that the prayers of this king, who now reigns with God, should be acceptable to him, since when he was a king on earth he always used to work and pray fervently for the eternal kingdom."[3]

This understanding of the place of burial being a place where the prayers of the saints in heaven had a strong effect was very much part of the earliest Christian tradition. When writing *Requiem Healing: A Christian Understanding*, I came across a number of catacomb inscriptions which reveal this early practice: For example, "Blessed Sozon gave back his soul aged 9 years. May the true Christ receive your spirit in peace, and pray for us," found on the catacomb of Gordian and Epimachus, sometime between 75–200 A.D.[4] This little prayer reveals that it was the custom to ask the dead to pray for the living. Burial places became special places, sanctified by the presence of the mortal remains of one who had been greatly loved in life, and was still loved in death. They were a connecting point between life and death, and an obvious place to not only remember the one who had died, but also to request their prayers for the living. In this way, there was an appropriate Christian interaction between living and dead which had nothing to do with superstition or spiritualism. However, it must be said that this practice did in time degenerate into cults of the dead and, in some situations, the dead saint became a kind of mini-god, and the burial place a worship shrine.

Cuthbert's Uncorrupted Body

Despite all the risks of cults of the dead developing, it seems that the Celtic Church fairly boldly accepted the practice of the infant church. Such cults probably did emerge, but they never seem to have been a serious threat in the Celtic Church. One person who must be mentioned in connection with this is Cuthbert. As we have already noted, Cuthbert was a man of outstanding Christian commitment, with roots deep in contemplative prayer and the hermit tradition, and with an evangelistic ministry which brought the gospel to thousands.

Cuthbert desired to spend his final years on his beloved Farne Island, living the life of a contemplative hermit, but he came under increasing pressure to give up his life of solitude to become a bishop. Eventually when none other than the king requested that he become bishop, Cuthbert was forced to move from his little island and become bishop of Lindisfarne, where he had two very remarkable years of pastoral and evangelistic ministry.

But it was not long before Cuthbert's body, which had been stretched to its very limits, became seriously weakened, and he became very ill. He was permitted to return to Farne Island where he died on 20 March 687 A.D. as the brothers around him, and those on Lindisfarne, were singing the Lauds. The body of Cuthbert was lovingly washed and dressed in his bishop's robes. It was covered in a shroud of waxed cloth and taken to Lindisfarne, where it was buried near the altar in the church. In modern Christian stories, that would be the final chapter, but that was not true with Cuthbert! For in Bede's *Life of Cuthbert*, we are given a number of well documented stories about healings happening at his tomb. For example, there was a demonized boy who was very distressed and violent. No one knew how to deliver him, not even one of the priests, who was particularly gifted in deliverance ministry. Then another of the priests was "instructed in spirit that Cuthbert could restore him to health." So he went off to where Cuthbert's body had been washed and found some of the earth where his water had fallen. He put this earth in the boy's mouth, and immediately, the violent boy with the roaring voice and bulging eyes was stilled and fell asleep. Bede tells us that he awoke from sleep to discover that "he had been freed from the spirit which had beset him through the prayers and merits of Cuthbert."[5]

Apart from various stories of this kind, there is one final and very extraordinary story about Cuthbert. Eleven years after Cuthbert's death, it was decided to exhume his body so that it could be placed in a new coffin above ground, where it would be more obvious for people to see. On the eleventh anniversary of his death, the original stone coffin was duly brought to the surface and opened. When they opened it, they were terrified—for therein the coffin was the uncorrupted body of Cuthbert! The body looked as if it were still alive, with the joints of the limbs still flexible, and the bishop's vestments were clean and "wonderfully bright." The frightened monks went off to Farne Island to collect Bishop Eadbert who was on a forty-day Lenten fast. He came immediately and said a beautiful prayer:

> What tongue can talk calmly about the gifts of God? What eye has ever seen the joys of Paradise? That will only be possible when we leave behind our earthly bodies and are received into the arc of Heaven by the Lord Himself. See how He honors the form of an earthly body in token of far greater glories to come! You have caused power to the dear bones of Cuthbert, Lord, filling the Church with the very atmosphere of Paradise. You

have bidden decay hold, as you did when you brought forth Jonah into the light of day after three days in the whale's belly. The tribe of Israel, which Pharaoh made to wander forty long years in the desert, you called to be your own people; you preserved Shadrach, Meshach, and Abednego in the flames of the fiery furnace and, when earth shall tremble at the last trump, you shall raise us to glory for your son's sake.[6]

Following this, Cuthbert's body was placed into its new coffin, along with a few of his personal belongings. The remains of this coffin, along with his pectoral cross, portable altar, and comb, which were buried with him, can now be seen in the Treasury of Durham Cathedral.

Anyone from an evangelical tradition will have great difficulty with these stories of miracles of healings by dead saints and uncorrupted bodies. It all seems too much like superstition, unbiblical practices of praying for the dead, and spiritualism. But before we pass judgment too quickly on the Celtic Church, we need to yet again go back to their time in history, long before the Protestant/Catholic battles of the sixteenth century and the Evangelical/Anglo-Catholic battles of this century. The Celtic Church was thoroughly opposed to any form of spiritualism, and, as Eadbert's prayer reveals, prayed only to God, not to the dead. So why did such things occur, these miracles "by the dead" and the uncorrupted body of Cuthbert?

The first thing we must remind ourselves of is the sanctity the Celts gave to "place." As we have already seen, the Celtic peoples had a great love for God's creation, and they believed it could be influenced for better or worse by spiritual presences. Because they did not have the separatist view that we have inherited of spirit-versus-matter, they were quite at ease with the notion that place and spirit could influence each other. Ground could be hallowed, and had to be prayed and fasted over before it could be used for a church or monastery.

The Celtic Church held a view that God liked to do special things in certain places, which then became "hallowed ground." Places like Lindisfarne still have a certain feel to them, which many of us sense when we go there. And so, when holy people died, and their bodies (which, remember, were not despised, but honored as a gift from God) were placed in the earth, that place became a place which marked a special work of God. Not only that, but it was a connecting point on earth, which brought together the worlds of heaven and earth. We have a real problem today in our clinical attitude towards death, whereby the body is seen as essentially a nasty embarrassment that must be disposed of as hygienically as possible, with a minimum of distress. This does not help the bereavement process, because deep within our souls, we have a need to find appropriate ways of not only honoring the body of the person who has died, but also of having a place to come to, which becomes a physical meeting point of earth and heaven. A healthy bereavement needs to have a "sure and certain hope" about eternal life and the freedom of the soul to go to Paradise after death, but we are also human beings who have a need to have on earth the things of heaven.

To some extent, the Celtic Church was using a Christian understanding of the dead to Christianize pagan beliefs about the dead. J.A. MacCulloch, in his *The Religion of the Ancient Celts*[7], devotes two chapters to the dead, in which he makes clear that the pre-Christian Celtic society was very aware of the presence of the dead. They were regularly remembered and had places laid for them with food and drink. On occasion, they needed to be appeased, especially if they had an untimely or violent death. A great commemoration of the dead was held on Samhain Eve. The Christian Church, as it emerged in this culture, took hold of this sharp awareness of the dead, and transformed it into something that was quite consistent with the Easter faith it proclaimed. The dead were real, but were not frightening. We could remember them, not to appease them, but to thank God for them. They were around, not to interfere in our lives, but to carry on their prayer life that began on earth. A new Christian festival of All Saints Day replaced the pagan festival at Samhain. All these customs were used to reinforce the immovable conviction of the resurrection of Jesus from the dead.

The uncorrupted body was a further potent symbol to the Celtic Church of the power of Jesus over death. The prayer of

Eadbert resounds with this hope. There is no suggestion whatsoever of cultic devotion to Cuthbert here, as Eadbert is caught up in a paean of praise to his Redeemer. The uncorrupted body was a true symbol of resurrection, a kind of parable of Romans 8:11: "If the Spirit of him who raised Jesus from the dead dwells in you, he who raised Christ from the dead will give life to your mortal bodies also through his Spirit who dwells in you." There is the sense that the Spirit of God was so active in Cuthbert's body that, for a time, not even the natural forces of earthly corruption could affect it. The body eventually did corrupt, but not for a long time. In 1104 it was taken to Durham, and in 1537 it was opened to Henry VIII's commissioners; both occasions revealed that the body was still uncorrupted. It was not until the investigation in 1827, that only the skeleton was found.

The Celtic Christian community clearly had a very positive view of death, and were great enthusiasts of heaven. There are many songs and hymns which speak with longing for that nearer presence of God. They also had a very healthy dread of hell, as the story of Drythelm makes very clear. They were very aware of the effects of sin, and preached salvation in Christ crucified. As we saw in the story of Chad, Celtic Christians were aware of the anger and judgment of God and would often pray for his mercy. Bede tells us a rather gruesome story of a layman who held a military post in the army of King Coenred in Mercia. He was fairly carefree and had been sinful in many ways. The king urged him to repent, but he would not. Even as he was dying, he was too proud to repent. Then, just before he died, he had a terrible vision in which he was shown by the devil a book of all his wicked deeds. Thus the man died in anguish of soul, and Bede reports, "So he is now vainly undergoing everlasting torments because he refused to undergo penance for a short while to win the grace of pardon."[8] Bede recorded one or two such stories and clearly used them to warn Christian people not to be presumptuous about their salvation, but to constantly remain open to God's grace through regular confession and forgiveness. In these days of easy-come and easy-go Christianity, we would do well to be challenged by these warnings.

Therefore, we find in the Celtic Church, a people who had a very holistic view of death, an appreciation of the communion of saints which was deeply encouraging, a vital hope of heaven, and a sober view of hell.

Bible Reading

1 Corinthians 15:12–58 The body will be raised to glory.

Questions for Reflection and Discussion

1. How do you feel about dying? (Be honest—many Christians are scared of dying, but find it hard to tell others because they they think *ought* not to fear it.) Allow God to speak to you about this.

2. Think of the Christian people you have loved who have died and are now part of the "company of witnesses" in heaven. If they are buried near you, perhaps you might like to visit their grave, thanking God for their lives, and becoming aware of their prayer for you.

3. How do you imagine heaven? Ask the Holy Spirit to inspire your mind as you contemplate this, and be open to his giving you visions of glory!

Prayer

Christ is risen. He is risen indeed, Alleluia!

Christ is risen from the stagnant ground:
Let all creation rise to greet his returning Splendor.
Christ is risen to tread down the powers of hell:
Let all who know loss and destruction rise to greet their returning
    Savior.
Christ is risen to renew the face of the earth:
Let all who are parched rise to greet their returning Spring.
Christ is risen to form a new people of love:
Let all who feel abandoned rise to greet their returning Spouse.

Christ is risen. He is risen indeed, Alleluia![9]

Notes

1. See Dr. Maurice Rawling's *Beyond Death's Door* (Nelson) and *Before Death Comes* (Sheldon Press); and Raymond Moody's *Life after Life* (Bantam). These are full of accounts of those who have returned from death experiences. Paul and Linda Badham's *Immortality or Extinction* (SPCK) is a much more scholarly work on the subject. See also *Requiem Healing* (Daybreak) by Russ Parker and myself.

2. David Adam, *The Cry of the Deer* (Triangle, 1987), p. 75.

3. Bede, *Ecclesiastical History*, p. 162.

4. Michael Mitton & Russ Parker, *Requiem Healing* (Daybreak, 1991), p. 52.

5. Bede, "Life of Cuthbert," in *The Age of Bede*, p. 95.

6. *The Age of Bede*, p. 97.

7. J.A. MacCulloch, *The Religion of the Ancient Celts* (Constable, first published 1911, paperback edition 1992), ch. 10, 22.

8. Bede, *Ecclesiastical History*, p. 209f.

9. *Morning Prayer in Celtic Tradition for Sundays and Eastertide*, St. Aidan Trust.

Chapter 8

The Mission
of Evangelism

Columbanus, Missionary and Evangelizer

Columbanus was born in Leinster, Ireland, in 540 A.D. As a young man he joined Comgall's monastery at Bangor, County Down, having heard the call to be a monk through a woman hermit. He was ordained in 572 A.D. and he developed a reputation for being a fine scholar, but within him was the urge to take the gospel overseas. Finally, in 591 A.D., when he was over 50 years old, he felt a clear call to carry the gospel to Gaul. There he discovered a number of Celtic settlements of British people who had fled the Anglo-Saxon invasions. He moved to Burgundy and settled in a narrow valley in the foothills of the Vosges, near the Swiss/German border, where he founded a monastic community. He built his first church on the site of the ruined temple of Diana, following the Celtic custom of redeeming land once devoted to pagan worship. From there he went on to establish another community in a discarded Roman fort at Luxeuil, where, as at Vosges, he and the community transformed a wild and barren land to a land of fruit orchards and cornfields.

Columbanus might well have settled in Luxeuil had he not fallen out of favor with the king of Burgundy. The King took exception to Columbanus, who had severely rebuked him for a wayward life that involved various mistresses and illegitimate children. He ordered Columbanus to return to Ireland, but when they boarded the ship on the Loire, a great tidal wave came up from the estuary. The sailors were terrified and refused to take Columbanus anywhere. Columbanus took this as a sign that he was not to return to Ireland, so, at the age of seventy, he began his wanderings again, traveling this time to Switzerland, where he settled for a time by Lake Constance. He immediately began evangelizing and sought to spiritually cleanse the area by chopping down sacred trees that had become occultic idols to the locals. This roused violent opposition from the locals, who forced Columbanus and his companions to flee over the Alps. After a short stay in Milan, they eventually settled in Bobbio, in Italy, where they built a monastery. Here Columbanus died on 23 November 615 A.D.

The story of Columbanus reveals many typical aspects of Celtic (particularly Irish Celtic) ways of mission, which were spontaneous, community based, prayerful, and fearless. Columbanus was more ascetic and more confrontational than some of the British Celtic missionaries, but they all shared the same passionate desire to evangelize the lost. What then were the keys to the success of the Celtic mission? I would suggest a number of factors.

Evangelism and Cultural Sensitivity

Firstly, there was a deep sensitivity about the way the Celtic Church went about its mission. Nowhere do you get the feel of a powerful ecclesiastical force moving in on reluctant individuals. They were not infected by the rather depressing doctrines of the loathsomeness of human beings that were starting to emanate from some parts of Europe; they held a much more optimistic view of human beings, who were, after all, made in the image of God. While the Celtic Church was very clear about the reality and consequence of human sin and was not shy in teaching about hell, it nonetheless seemed to have had a reasonably positive view about human nature, just as it had a positive view about God's good creation; the two were very much connected. God's created order was damaged, but not completely. So individuals, the land they lived on, the communities that they were part of, and the way they lived were to be respected.

Aidan set a fine example in this respect. Bede tells us that Chad traveled on foot and not on horseback when he went to preach the Gospel, whether in towns or countries, in cottages, villages, or strongholds; for he was one of Aidan's disciples and always sought to instruct his people by the same methods as Aidan and his own brother, Cedd.[1] Aidan's influence of gentleness seems to have been far reaching, which is in contrast to many forms of mission that have been used in and from this country subsequently. Ian Bradley writes:

> The way that they worked was very different from the approach of later Christian missionaries who joined forces with traders and imperial adventurers and sought to impose their

own Western values and secure a cultural as well as a religious conversion of the natives.... The approach of the Celtic missionaries was essentially gentle and sensitive. They sought to live alongside the people with whom they wanted to share the good news of Christ, to understand and respect their beliefs and not to dominate or culturally condition them.[2]

All this was very different from the presentations of the gospel that had come with the Roman Christian legionaries, whose influence in the country was minimal. "This time it was not grand governors riding in elegant chariots who carried the gospel," writes Robert Van de Weyer, "but barefoot monks plodding the muddy lanes."[3]

A fine example of this was Cuthbert. When Boisil died, Cuthbert became prior of the monastery at Melrose, and we are told by Bede that Cuthbert carried out this office "with holy zeal." He spent part of his time in the monastery in his ministry of teaching and prayer, but often he would follow the example of Boisil and venture out from this community on evangelistic expeditions. In his travels it seems Cuthbert encountered many people who had strayed from the faith into all kinds of superstitions, which Bede graphically described as "diabolical rubbish!" Cuthbert's way of evangelizing was to travel to a village, sometimes on horseback, but usually on foot, and upon arriving at the village, to begin preaching.

The church had very quickly made an impact on the people of Northumbria and, by Cuthbert's time, villagers would have recognized a Christian preacher, and they would have gathered around and listened. Bede tells us of Cuthbert, "Such was his skill in teaching, such his power of driving his lessons home, and so gloriously did his angelic countenance shine forth, that none dared keep back from him even the closest secrets of their heart."[4] But Cuthbert did not go just to the established village communities. He went up into the hills where apparently other preachers dreaded going because there lived small groups of the very poor, whom most tried to avoid because of their squalor. Cuthbert would quite often disappear into the hills to live among these people, sometimes for up to a month, before returning to Melrose again.

Cuthbert continued this evangelistic ministry after his time on Farne Island as a hermit, and he used the opportunity of his ministry as a bishop to once again travel far and wide, as he did at Melrose, preaching the gospel and healing the sick. For him, as for all Celtic bishops, his ministry was not simply to the church, it was a missionary ministry which he fulfilled with great devotion until his death in 687.

Very important to Celtic mission was the spiritual gift of discernment (1 Cor. 12:10). Because the Celtic Church invested so much in a prayerful opening up of the intuitive and imaginative to the influence of the Holy Spirit, they were very sensitive to the presence of good and evil in people and places. They therefore sensed what was good in a community and blessed it accordingly, or they sensed evil, in which case they combated it in prayer. On some occasions, especially with Columba and Patrick, we find that these combats gained almost Mount Carmel-like proportions as, in the spirit of Elijah, they challenged the occultic powers of particularly dark druids. But this kind of contest was not common, and much of what they found in the communities they evangelized were things they could either bless or Christianize.

When they began to evangelize my home county of Derbyshire, for example, they discovered the custom in a village of worshiping water divinities at the rivers and wells. Various divinities were honored at these water places. When the Christians came they did not attack these customs. They did not do dazzling exorcisms and engage in glorious victories over the enemy, as would happen in some charismatic circles today where any whiff of the demonic is attacked with great gusto. Such battles can often be due to our own needs for power, rather than to the presence of spiritual conflict, and the Celtic communities were deeply suspicious of Christian power games. Rather, they would listen carefully to the community's deep need to give thanks for the gift of water; and so they would bless their need to give thanks for and honor the gift of water, while at the same time, proclaiming the cross of Christ over the place and making clear the need for redemption. I am sure in some cases, where they discerned the site had been spoiled in some way by dark powers, this would have involved some kind of exorcistic ministry with fasting and prayer.

And that is why, in Derbyshire, we find that a number of wells have changed names, often with such subtlety that the names stayed almost the same. For example, a well once dedicated to the water sprite Eilan, was now dedicated to St. Helen. The Celts also encouraged the custom of annual thanksgiving for water, and the primitive pagan well-dressing ceremonies became Christian ceremonies. These ceremonies are very popular today in many Derbyshire towns and villages, where you can find town and village festivals centered around wonderfully decorated wells, usually depicting a biblical theme.

All this seems very risky, for surely there is a real danger of syncretism. But the Celtic Church did not fear this because it was so deeply rooted in the word of God and knew the vibrancy of the power of the Spirit. The Celtic peoples had great confidence that their love for Jesus and his word would prevent them from straying into forbidden territories. They had great confidence that the Holy Spirit would give them the discernment to realize any tendency to return to evil. Where necessary, they did engage in fairly drastic measures, as in the case of Columbanus, who destroyed the occultic trees in Switzerland. In that case, it is no doubt that the trees had been carved and used in such a way that it was impossible to restore them to their original condition. But generally, the Celtic evangelists sought to redeem and reform. They really had much more confidence in the Word and the Spirit than those charismatic evangelicals today, who are very fearful of any attempt to understand New Age groups and modern forms of paganism. We can learn much from the Celtic Church's confidence here, a confidence which enabled it to listen rather than dominate, a confidence that could discern when to Christianize, and when to confront dark powers.

Evangelism and Power

The second important feature of Celtic evangelism has to do with their understanding of power. We will look at this more fully in a later chapter, but it does need to be mentioned here because it was an important feature of Celtic evangelism. Many of the stories of the miraculous were in the context of mission, the Celtic Church would have been quite at home with John Wimber's phrase "Power Evangelism." The Celtic peoples of the time would have had no difficulty with the concept of supernatural power; their concerns would be where it came from, and why it was being used.

In reading the stories of the Celtic mission, it is clear that the power of the Spirit was closely linked with personal holiness and with remarkable humility. They no doubt felt a strong affinity with St. Paul, who wrote to the Corinthian Church, "And I came to you in weakness and in fear and with much trembling. My speech and my proclamation were not with plausible words of wisdom, but with a demonstration of the Spirit and of power" (1 Cor. 2:3,4).

By its humility and authenticity, the church showed that it was interested in using this power not for dominance, but genuinely, to demonstrate that the love of God could have a powerful effect on people's lives and could rescue, heal, and deliver them. This belief challenges the unbelief in the church today, which is only just beginning to emerge from the cold grip of rationalism. It also challenges the tendency of many charismatic churches who have discovered the power of God, but who keep it confined to the church in healing services and conferences. And finally, it challenges those who do practice a healing and deliverance ministry at evangelistic meetings, but who do it in a style which is too closely connected with styles and images of human powers—the extrovert evangelist with loud voice and garish suit, backed up by an imposing platform party, communicates a message much more to do with human manipulation, than the demonstration of the power of God through human weakness.

Evangelism and Community

A third feature of the Celtic Church's evangelism was its community base, which we have already discussed in Chapter 4. These monastic communities were not only places to which interested people could come and investigate the faith; they also became schools and universities, hospitals, and centers for social care of all kinds, thus drawing in large numbers of non-Christian people who encountered a community with a living faith in God. Furthermore, these communities acted as mission stations which trained men and women in preaching and healing, and sent them out on missions. Many of those who went out from the communities did not return; they formed other communities which were made up of newly converted people. Sometimes individuals would go out on their own to live a hermit life, but, as happened in the deserts of Egypt, others would come and gather near their hut or cave, and a small community would develop. The church grew quickly because these cells were so wonderfully flexible and unrestrained by any institution, that they could easily multiply.

Some, like Chad's brother Cedd, seemed to have a particular ministry of church and monastery establishment. Consecrated as bishop of the East Saxons, he set up a number of churches and communities in his evangelistic work among the East Saxons. Bede records, "To the great joy of the king and all the people, the Gospel of eternal life made daily headway throughout the province for a considerable time."[5] There is no doubt that the network of evangelistic communities had an immense impact.

One of the reasons why the community base was so important is that it provided great security in a society that was deeply troubled and constantly under threat. With the collapsing of Roman civilization, which had been so secure for so long, and the new civilizations of the Angles, Saxons, and Jutes pushing in from the East, it was a time of massive cultural change; and these little communities provided an oasis of security. There are examples of this need for security in Western society today. With the prevailing culture of the Enlightenment Era collapsing, and with all kinds of new influences coming in from many different directions, there are increasing signs of profound anxiety in our culture. In addition to this, the previously strong nuclear community unit of the family is under great threat; and our attempts at wider unity, such as the European Community, seem to constantly founder. But God has put it into the heart of all people to belong to community, for we are made in the image of God, who is a community of the Holy Trinity. Essential to our proclamation of the good news, therefore, is that we proclaim a community that is based not on values of ideology, consumerism, or rationalism, but rather, on the counterculture of the sermon on the mount.

John Finney, the bishop of Pontefract, carried out a detailed piece of research during the 1980s, investigating how people come to faith. The fruits of this research can be found in his book, *Finding Faith Today*, which was published in 1992. One of the discoveries of his research was that, "for most people the corporate life of the church is a vital element in the process of becoming a Christian and for about a quarter it is the vital factor." He adds the stark comment, "Forms of evangelism which fail to recognize this are doomed."[6] Although we may be a thousand years on from the days of the early Celtic Church, we nonetheless find that it says something vital to us about community and evangelism today.

Evangelism and Abandonment

The fourth feature of Celtic evangelism that we should take note of was its wonderful sense of joyful abandonment. Few Celtic missions were formally planned. Instead, they involved setting off from the community, asking God to direct their steps, and being open to his surprises. Aidan's way of evangelizing was typical: "Whether in town or country, he always traveled on foot unless compelled by necessity to ride; and whatever people he met on his walks, whether high or low, he stopped and spoke to them. If they were heathen he urged them to be baptized; and if they were Christians he strengthened their faith."[7]

People like Aidan would return in due course to their community. But others, like Columbanus, were willing to venture out even to far off lands, not knowing where they would end up. These people were called *peregrinati*, or "perpetual wanderers."

The fundamental difference between the early Celtic Church and the established churches of Britain and Ireland today is that the Celtic Church was utterly dedicated to mission. It thought, lived, and breathed mission and could understand no Christianity that did not include mission. The Celtic Church had no interest in bureaucracies and institutions that existed simply to support the church. It had a wild, childlike, simple, and overwhelming passion to see the men, women, and children of its lands and beyond find faith in Jesus Christ. If nothing else compels us to respect this church, that feature of its life commands our respect. In our spiritual roots of Christian faith, we have a sensitive, powerful, community-based, carefree mission church. Perhaps this church, more than any other, discovered what God has truly given us—a missionary responsibility that has nothing to do with the imposition of Western culture and manipulation, but has to do with a humble, foolish abandonment to the gospel of the Lord Jesus, who died, who was raised, and who sits at the right hand of God.

Bible Reading
1 Corinthians 2:1–5 The gospel, human weakness, and the power of God.

Questions for Reflection and Discussion
1. How sensitive is the evangelism of your church? What parts of the culture around your church deserve your blessing? What parts need to be challenged? How can you go about affirming the good and challenging the bad? Are there aspects of life in your local community that you could Christianize in some way?

2. How much of a community is your local church? How evangelistically effective is the community life of your church? Is the quality of life in your church community better than in the secular community around it? If so, what are the differences? If not, why not?

3. In what way can you be like the *peregrinati*? Why don't

you try wandering out into the neighborhood to see who God causes you to meet. Can you think of ways in which your church can engage more in this carefree evangelism?

Pꞧayeꞧ
Prayer of St. Columba

Kindle in our hearts, O God,
The flame of that love which never ceases,
That it may burn in us giving light to others.
May we shine forever in your holy temple,
Set on fire with your eternal light,
Even your son Jesus Christ,
Our savior and redeemer.[8]

Notes
1. *The Age of Bede*, ch. 9.
   2. Ian Bradley, *The Celtic Way*, p. 74f.
   3. Robert Van de Weyer, *Celtic Fire*.
   4. Bede, *Ecclesiastical History*, p. 197.
   5. Bede, *Ecclesiastical History*, p. 180.
   6. John Finney, *Finding Faith Today* (Bible Society, 1992), p. 43.
   7. Bede, *Ecclesiastical History*, p. 150.
   8. *The Vigil of Fire*, St. Aidan Trust.

Chapter 9

Healing
and the Miraculous

John of Beverley, Bishop of Hexham

I n 685 A.D., a man known as John of Beverley, was made
Bishop of Hexham. By any standards he was a remarkable
person, overflowing with the Holy Spirit in such abundance that miracles occurred fairly regularly in his ministry.
The key to this was his habit of taking time away from his active ministry to reflect and pray. Bede tells us that "whenever
opportunity offered, and especially during Lent, this man of
God used to retire with a few companions to read and pray
quietly in an isolated house surrounded by open woodland
and a dyke."[1] This was about a mile away from the church at
Hexham across the river Tyne. One Lent, John went there
with his companions for his lenten retreat, and, as was his
habit, he sent his companions to go and find some person in
need and invite them to spend Lent with them in their prayerful little community. When the group went out on their
search, they came to a village where they found a dumb
youth, whom John had already met on his visits there. This
poor boy was not only afflicted with dumbness, but he also
had a serious skin disease, which was so bad on his scalp that
he had lost most of his hair. The boy gladly agreed to come
and join this community for Lent.

After about a week, John decided it was time to begin helping this lad, so he called him and asked him to stick out his
tongue. The boy duly obeyed, and John gently held his chin
and then made the sign of the cross on his tongue. "Now say a
word, say 'yes,'" he said, and the amazed boy found he could
say "yes." Slowly and painstakingly, John went through the
alphabet, helping him to pronounce all the letters. He then
taught the boy many words, all of which he was delighted to
learn. Eventually, the boy was speaking in full sentences. The
floodgates were now open, and the boy did not stop talking
all the rest of the day and all night! Bede remarks that he was
like the lame man healed by Peter and John, who could not
stop walking and leaping and praising God. In the same way
this boy delighted in his new found power of speech.

But the boy still had his terrible skin problem. For this,

John decided to consult a doctor and "with the assistance of the bishop's blessing and prayer," the skin healed and new hair started to grow back on his head. By Easter day, a very happy young boy left the community, with clear skin, a thick head of hair, and fluent speech.

This story is an excellent example of the way the Celtic Church went about its healing ministry. In this story we see a number of important features that were essential to the Celtic Church's understanding of healing and the miraculous.

A Goð of the Miraculous

First, we see that the Celtic Church was quite at ease with God intervening miraculously in the lives of the faithful. There was no sense of dispensationalism, which says that the gifts of the Spirit are simply for the apostolic age. D.H. Farmer, in his introduction to the Penguin version of Bede's *Ecclesiastical History*, writes:

> It is unsurprising that Bede's *History* contains miracle stories. Not all have the same explanation: Some were probably the result of natural forces, psychological factors, or apparent coincidence. But all contained some marvelous element *(mirum)* which revealed God's power and care. Some of the stories reveal significant detail of interest to the historian. Although many of them seem to be a stumbling block to the modern reader, their absence would have been an even greater difficulty to Bede's contemporaries.[2]

There was a very high expectation that holy people would be ready vehicles through which God could work powerfully. Bede took great care to give authentication of the miracles. He often gave the name of the person who witnessed the miracle, or who heard the story first-hand, so the contemporary reader could carry out further investigation. Thus, for example, the story related above was one of several stories about John told by a man called Berthun, who was John's deacon, but was abbot of the monastery at In-Derawuda at the time he wrote the stories. Anyone could have gone to Berthun to have him personally authenticate such stories.

At the end of the seventh century, Adomnan, abbot of Iona,

was the celebrated author of the biography of Columba, which gives a great deal of attention to the many miracles God performed through Columba. Although the duke of Argyll, who wrote in the last century, talked about "the atmosphere of miracles" that pervaded the island of Iona during Columba's time, it is generally believed that many of the miracle stories surrounding Columba's ministry were either exaggerated or sheer fabrication. For example, Columba was even purported to have seen the Loch Ness Monster. It was customary among the Celts to commemorate great men by exaggerating their deeds, but even allowing for this, there was a great deal of miraculous activity in those early days of the community at Iona. Ian Finlay's *Columba* is well recognized as a thorough piece of work on Columba's life and ministry; and, while he is dismissive of a fair proportion of these miracles, he concedes, "Columba must have been a man endowed with immense authority and personal magnetism, and I would certainly accept he had the ability to heal by faith and prayer, the more so since he was among men and women who had never doubted his powers."[3]

It has been the custom in academic circles in the twentieth century to "demythologize" stories that include the miraculous. But as we approach the twenty-first century and leave the Enlightenment era, there is increasing openness to accepting the miraculous, partly because of the emergence of some very able Pentecostal theologians, who are writing from their experience of the miraculous. This was exactly the situation that the Celtic theologians found themselves in—they witnessed God working in marvelous ways, and they reflected theologically on it. Mark Stibbe, a charismatic theologian, writes: "Celtic Christians would have been more than happy with Westerhoff's circle of theological learning, which comprises experience, reflection, and action. For them, an ongoing experience of the supernatural meant that the kind of anti-supernatural bias which we see in most recent theology was unthinkable. Their experience of the Spirit made such rational skepticism an impossibility."[4]

Healing anð Holíness

Secondly, we learn from this story that the miraculous is closely linked with holiness and prayer. In the 1980s, many churches were helped into the healing ministry through the teaching and "healing clinics" of John Wimber. Many of us are greatly indebted to John Wimber for the way he has helped so many churches incorporate healing into normal church life, rather than as a specialist ministry for the "experts." I am not sure to what extent the Celtic Church would have expected *everyone* to engage in the healing ministry. It does seem to have been mainly confined to certain Christian leaders. Perhaps this is an area in which they would have learned from today's church. But what we do learn from the Celtic Church, is that God's power moved through John and Columba because they were deeply prayerful people. One of the dangers of widening the healing ministry to involve all is that we can too easily forget that we need to prepare ourselves in prayer and become open to God's power through living holy lives. As we know from St. Paul, it is possible to do all kinds of miraculous things without love (1 Cor. 13:1–3), but, in doing so, nothing is gained. Miracles in themselves have no great value. It is when they are connected to lives which transparently reveal the love of God, that they draw people into the kingdom of God.

There is also no doubt that the Celtic Church believed deep intercessory prayer was needed for some healings. Another story of John of Beverley illustrates this fact. We have in Bede's *History* a first-hand account of a healing of a priest called Heribald, who fell from a horse while he was carelessly racing it. After the fall he was unable to move and lay "as though dead" with a cracked skull. He was very ill during the night, vomiting blood. Heribald tells us through Bede:

> The bishop was greatly distressed about my accident and possible death, because he was especially fond of me; and he did not remain with his clergy that night as was his custom, but spent all night in vigil and prayer, as I understand, asking God of His mercy to restore me to health. Early [the] next morning he came and said a prayer over me, calling me by name, and waking me out of what seemed to be a healing sleep. "Do you

know who it is who is speaking to you?" he asked. Opening my eyes, I replied: "I do. You are my beloved bishop." "Can you live?" he asked. "I can do so with the help of your prayers, God willing," I replied.[5]

We are told that Bishop John then laid his hands on his head and prayed for him, then went off again to pray some more. Heribald immediately began to recover, and by the next day, he was riding again. There was no doubt in Heribald's mind that he owed his life to the prayers of Bishop John. We also get some insight into the affection that existed between John and his clergy.

Healing and the Poor

A third lesson we learn from the story of John and the dumb boy is that the Celtic Church had a clear sense that the ministry of healing was especially appropriate among the poor. John wanted to find one of the poor and outcast with whom to share Lent. When Cuthbert was a bishop and, as was his custom, was visiting the very poor up in the hills, he held a confirmation service. In the middle of the service, some women brought in a young man who had some kind of wasting disease. Bede tells us that the youth was brought to Cuthbert who "had resource to his usual armory, prayer, and gave a blessing, and drove away the disease [for] which the doctors, despite their skill concocting medicines, had been unable to devise a cure."[6] The Celtic Church could always be found among the poor, and it was here that it delighted to proclaim by words and works, the loving mercy of God.

Holistic Healing

Finally, the opening story illustrates just how holistic the Celtic healing ministry was. John was as happy with prayer for the miraculous as he was with employing the services of a doctor. There is no sense in this story that the "spiritual" way is better. It would not have occurred to the Celtic Church to make much of a distinction—they would have recognized the healing of God in the work of the doctor. We are children of the age of scientific rationalism, which loves to dissect everything and to work out exactly which part is supernatural and which part is natural. There is no way of discerning this in many of the Celtic healing stories. Perhaps John was simply a good psychiatrist and helped the boy get over a phobia that had prevented him from using his tongue. Perhaps it was supernatural power. Only we, with our present-day mindset, would want to investigate this. For the Celtic Church it was a non-issue.

Of course, some miracles were so extraordinary that there could be no "rational explanation." There is another very touching story of Cuthbert, who, again on his travels as a bishop, came across a mother who was in great agony. She had already lost one son to the plague, and now her other little boy was dying in her arms. Cuthbert went up to her and kissed the boy, which was a very risky thing to do because the plague was so contagious, and then blessed him, saying "have no fear, do not grieve, the child will get better and live." Sure enough, he did, and there can be little doubt that it was a supernatural healing that saved him. But there is no sense that this kind of miracle was greater than the other. If the church today can regain this holistic approach to healing, we may become much more open to the full range of healing that God longs to give to this world.

Another form of healing that should be mentioned has to do with deliverance ministry. The Celtic Church had a clear understanding of the presence of angels and demons, and they knew that demons were sometimes responsible for causing personal distress and illness. But again, deliverance ministry was very much regarded as a part of the Celtic Church, and was not relegated to being a specialist ministry. It was, for the most part, done by those who were the most prayerful and holy. Cuthbert in particular seems to have had a very effective deliverance ministry. On one occasion, Cuthbert was called to bring emergency deliverance to the wife of a sheriff called Hildmer. This lady was a Christian but was "suddenly possessed of a devil" (which is an interesting point to note for those who are engaged in the discussions concerning whether or not Christians can be demonized). Hildmer came to

Cuthbert greatly distressed, thinking that his wife was dying, but Cuthbert was confident she would be released. They rode together to her home, and as they approached the house, the evil spirit in the woman, "unable to bear the coming of the Holy Spirit with whom Cuthbert was filled, suddenly departed." The woman was instantly cured.[7] There are no theatricals here—it is all wonderfully straightforward!

Not all miracles were to do with healing. There are stories of Aidan pouring oil on a very rough sea to save some monks, whose boat was in difficulty and were at risk of drowning—the waters calmed after he had poured the oil out. There are also various stories of miraculous events at the mixed community in Barking. Bede calls them "proofs of holiness," which is probably a fairly accurate assessment. There is a curious and rather lovely story about this community. There was a time when many men in the community were dying of the plague. The women knew that it was only a matter of time before they would be affected, and the mother of the community started to make plans for their burial. But they could not decide where they wanted to be buried. Then, one night, after they had sung their psalms, they went out, as usual, to visit the graveyard where the brothers who had died were buried. Here, in the darkness, they sang praises to God and suddenly "a light from heaven like a great sheet suddenly appeared and shone over them all, so alarming that they even broke off their singing in consternation." It was a brilliant light, brighter than the midday sun, and after a while it rose up and traveled to the south side of the convent, hovered there for a while, and then went back up to heaven. UFO spotters would have been most excited by this! However, the nuns had no doubt that it was a signal from heaven as to where their bodies should lie after their death.[8] This story tells us so much about the nuns' positive attitude to death; about how they mourned for their brothers; about their openness to the supernatural intervention of God. It also tells us that God delights to speak to us about the things that concern us, and he may even do it in miraculous ways.

But we should finally note that, although there were many

signs of the miraculous activity of God around at that time, there was not the expectation that all would be healed and delivered miraculously from their difficulties. The mother of the Barking community, Ethelburga, was ill for nine years with a sickness that caused her great distress. Bede clearly understands that this illness was allowed for purgatorial reasons, that her strength might be made perfect in weakness, and "that any traces of sin that remained among her virtues through ignorance or neglect might be burned away in the fires of prolonged suffering."[9] There was an understanding that illness could serve some kind of purgatorial work on earth. Cuthbert, who was so ill just before Boisil died, carried a nagging pain in his leg from that illness for the rest of his life. There is no suggestion in the Celtic Church of pressure being put on people if they were not healed. They were beautifully open to God, walking whichever pathway he chose for them.

Bible Reading
Luke 10:1–12 Jesus commissions his disciples for healing.

Questions for Reflection and Discussion
1. Do you have any difficulty in accepting that God works miraculously in this world? If so, why? Have you had the experience of seeing him work miraculously in your life or someone else's? How can you be more open to his working in this way?

2. Think about the holistic approach of the Celtic Church to healing. Does this challenge or confirm the way that the healing ministry is encouraged in your church?

3. Is there someone you could be praying for who needs healing? Spend some time listening to God to see how he might want to use you in this way. Pray that those you know who are sick, especially those like Ethelburga who have been sick for a long time, will know the strength of God in their weakness.

Prayer
A Prayer following Communion

Heaven is intertwined with earth. Alleluia!
We have taken the divine life into ourselves. Alleluia!
And so now each may say,
I rise up clothed in the strength of Christ.
I shall not be imprisoned, I shall not be harmed;
I shall not be downtrodden, I shall not be left alone;
I shall not be tainted, I shall not be overwhelmed.
I go clothed in Christ's white garments;
I go freed to weave Christ's patterns;
I go loved to serve Christ's weak ones;
I go armed to rout Christ's foes.[10]

Notes
1. Bede, *Ecclesiastical History*, p. 267.
   2. Bede, *Ecclesiastical History*, p. 26f.
   3. Ian Finlay, *Columba* (London: Gollancz Ltd., 1979), p. 173.
   4. Mark Stibbe, "The Revival of Anglican Theology: Lessons from Celtic Christianity," *Anglicans for Renewal*, (Spring 1994): vol. 56.
   5. Bede, *Ecclesiastical History*, p. 274.
   6. *The Age of Bede*, ch. 32, p. 83.
   7. *The Age of Bede*, p. 61f.
   8. Bede, *Ecclesiastical History*, p. 217f.
   9. Bede, *Ecclesiastical History*, p. 219.
   10. *A Eucharist in the Celtic Tradition*, St. Aidan Trust.

Chapter 10

Ministry of Women

Brigíd, Abbess of Kíldare

In 455 A.D., during the early days of the Christian mission in Ireland, a girl was born who was to become one of the greatest saints in the Celtic Church. Her father was Dubtach, the king of Leinster. Her mother, a Christian called Broisseach, was a bondwoman of the king. Shortly before Broisseach gave birth to a child, he sold her to a druid priest. So it was that Brigid (or Brigit) was born to a Christian mother in a pagan household. There was something special about Brigid from her earliest days. She was apparently baptized by Patrick, who no doubt discerned the call of God on her life.

Some years later the king decided to have his daughter back in the palace, but he soon regretted it because Brigid had the annoying habit of constantly giving away food and goods to the poor! By the time she was fourteen, Dubtach could stand it no longer, so he decided to marry her off to a nobleman nearby. Brigid stubbornly refused, and instead opted to become a nun. It seems the king had no objections to this, and the young Brigid embarked on a remarkable ministry.

Her strong-willed and buoyant personality soon led to the founding of her own community. She needed to find some land for this, and she appealed to the local chief for a small plot. He refused. Characteristically Brigid persevered, eventually getting him to agree to a piece of land that was no bigger than the size of her cloak. He was astonished, however, to find that when Brigid laid her cloak on the grass, it grew until it covered the whole of the Curragh, the grassy plain to the east of Kildare! It was here that one of the most famous communities of Ireland was founded, and Brigid became the Abbess. Kildare was famed for its magical oak trees which were very special to the druids, but Brigid's community turned it into a center where Christ was exalted, and the light of the gospel shone from this community to the pagan world around it. Brigid lit a fire at the center of this community as a sign of this light. Only women were allowed to attend this fire, and it remained alight for a thousand years, until the dissolution of the monasteries.

Brigid remained based at this community for the rest of her life and died around 523 A.D. Later her remains were taken to be placed alongside Patrick's in Downpatrick. Ireland has traditionally respected Patrick and Brigid as their two greatest evangelists.

There were a number of fundamental differences between Celtic society and other European societies, and one of these was in the attitude toward women. Peter Beresford Ellis writes:

> The status of women in Celtic society and their social prominence has been found remarkable by many scholars. The female had a unique place in the Celtic world compared with other civilizations. She was regarded equally and could be elected as chief; she could, and did, lead her tribe as military commander—as the Icenian Boudicca did in 60 A.D. Celtic women enjoyed an equality of rights which would have been envied by their Roman sisters.[1]

In Roman society, when a woman married she, along with all her goods, effectively became a belonging of the man's family. By law, she could own no property. In Celtic society the woman very much retained her identity, and there was no sense of the husband owning her or her belongings. Celtic women continued to personally own anything they brought into the marriage, and the husband had no rights over their property. Nora Chadwick, in *The Celts*, informs us that "an interesting feature of Pictish institutions was inheritance through the female."[2] All of this, of course, needs to be seen in the context of the close community in which the Celts lived. The tribe would live as a close knit family, in which household duties were shared. Both parents took responsibility for raising the children, and both parents were free to follow their work, leaving the children safely in the care of the tribe. It was perhaps the community nature of Celtic life that was the key to enabling women to enjoy a freedom that was denied them in other cultures which were more individualistic.

It was therefore inevitable that the emerging Christian Church would take this positive attitude toward women into their community life. Thus there was no problem for women like Brigid, Hilda, Ebba, Ethelburga, or others exercising leadership roles in their communities. Again, because there was a strong sense of equality within the community, issues to do with rights of women do not seem to have been an issue. Brigid clearly had a well respected and accepted role as abbess of her community at Kildare. The community at Kildare contained both men and women and, as Shirley Toulson points out, as a manager "Brigid must have shown the organizing ability, energy, and commonsense of Teresa of Avila, who also combined worldly wisdom with spiritual insights."[3]

Mary Calvert, writing about Brigid, informs us, "Brigid needed priests to perform the offices which no woman was allowed to.... She selected Conleath to be the bishop who 'in episcopal dignity' would govern with her, but as to who actually ruled the abbey, there was never any real doubt!"[4]

I have not yet discovered any discussion in early Celtic literature to inform us if there was any debate in which leaders like Brigid were seeking ordination. However, there is one legendary tale which suggests that there were some who would have been very comfortable not only with the idea of Brigid being a priest, but of her being a bishop. Christopher Bamford and William Parker Marsh record for us the story of her visit to Telcha Mide with a number of other women for a service of "taking the veil" led by Bishop Mel. During the course of this, a strange phenomenon took place:

> A fiery pillar arose from her head to the roof-ridge of the church. Then said Bishop Mel: "Come, O holy Brigid, that a veil may be sained on thy head before the other virgins."
> It came to pass then, through the grace of the Holy Ghost, that the form of ordaining a Bishop was read over Brigid. Mac-Caille said that a bishop's order should not be conferred on a woman. Said Bishop Mel: "No power have I in this matter. That dignity hath been given by God unto Brigid, beyond every woman." Wherefore the men of Ireland from that time to this give episcopal honor to Brigid's successor.[5]

Whatever we make of a story like this, it tells us that there existed a tradition that deeply respected Brigid and would have had no objection had heaven decided to consecrate her as a bishop.

Hilda of Whitby

Brigid's community in Ireland must have been an inspiration to Hilda, a much loved English Celtic saint. Hilda had a very different personality than did Brigid. Brigid had a lot of fight in her and was a leader because she was headstrong and determined, characteristics that God made wonderful use of at Kildare. Hilda was more of an intellectual and a diplomat.

Like Brigid, she was born into a royal family. She was the daughter of Hereric, nephew to King Edwin. Her mother was Breguswith who, one night when Hilda was an infant, had a dream. In this dream Hereric was suddenly taken away from her and, although she searched everywhere for him, she could not find him. But, at the end of her searching, she did find something quite unexpected. Bede tells us, "she discovered a most valuable jewel under her garments; and as she looked closely, it emitted such a brilliant light that all Britain was lit by its splendor."[6] Breguswith did lose her husband shortly afterwards when he was poisoned in a political intrigue, but she had discovered a jewel: her daughter. The dream was certainly prophetic, for Hilda was a jewel that brightened all of Britain.

Hilda was baptized by Bishop Paulinus in 627 A.D., when she was thirteen years old. Bede tells us that her life neatly fit into two parts: she spent thirty-three years "most nobly in secular occupations," followed by thirty-three years in the monastic life. It was Aidan who encouraged her into ministry, no doubt influenced by the way that the ministry of women had been developed in the communities in Ireland where he had come from. Aidan had already appointed Ebba to found a convent at Coldingham, near Berwick in about 540 A.D. Her niece, Elfleda, also had a very distinguished ministry, and she eventually became abbess at Whitby. But Hilda was the most famous of Aidan's disciples. In 649 A.D. he persuaded her to establish a monastery at Hartlepool for men and women. She had not been there long before she moved, with characteristic Celtic restlessness, to form another community, this time at Tadcaster.

She remained in Tadcaster before she founded the monastery for which she became famous. This was at a place called Straenaeshalch, which we now call Whitby. Bede writes of her ministry here:

> She established the same regular life as in her former monastery, and taught the observance of righteousness, mercy, purity, and other virtues, but especially of peace and charity. After the example of the primitive Church, no one there was rich, no one was greedy, for everything was held in common, and nothing was considered to be anyone's personal property. So great was her prudence that not only ordinary folk, but kings and princes used to come and ask her advice in their difficulties and take it. Those under her direction were required to make a thorough study of the Scriptures and occupy themselves in good works, to such good effect that many were found fitted for Holy Orders and the service of God's altar.[7]

It was clearly an extraordinary community, constantly training men and women for ministry. Five men from this monastery, including John of Beverley and the famous Wilfrid (who was later to champion the Roman way) became bishops. But the clerics were deemed no more important than the lay people, as we have seen in the story of Caedmon. It was at Whitby that the famous Synod was held in 664 A.D. to determine the future direction for the British Church. Hilda was probably very much involved at this tense conference in a conciliatory way, trying to hold the two groups, Roman and Celtic, together. But it must have saddened her deeply to see the decision go to the Romans, for she was very Celtic. She must also have had grave misgivings about the Roman view of women, which was far more oppressive than that of the Celts.

Towards the end of her life, Hilda became very ill and she was racked by a fever for six years. Despite the fact that stories of miraculous healing abounded all around her, Hilda was not cured of her physical ailment, but bore it courageously and was a great example to others in the community. Eventually, on 17 November 680 A.D., Hilda, to use the words of Bede, "joyfully welcomed death." The evening she died, in a new monastery a few miles away that she had only recently founded, a nun named Begu was sleeping in her dormitory when she heard the sound of a bell, the bell that was sounded when someone died. She opened her eyes and saw a vision of the roof opening and a great light flooding into the room. When she gazed into this light, she saw the soul of Hilda being taken up into heaven by several angels.[8]

The Celtic Church and Human Sexuality

What we find in the Celtic Church is a strong community context in which men and women worked happily together. Many monastic communities contained men and women, and many engaged in close and meaningful relationships with one another, apparently free of the Roman fear that any such friendships would sooner or late denigrate into lustful ways. Thus Brigid and Conleath, Aidan and Hilda, and Cuthbert and Aelfflaed could all enjoy useful and affectionate working relationships. The Celtic creation-affirming approach to life was largely responsible for this. The Roman Church, influenced by the post-Augustinian attitude which considered human nature to be depraved, had a very pessimistic view of human nature, and saw the need to guard against its weaknesses. The Celtic Church always had a more positive view of human nature, and, in many ways, seemed to be much more at ease with human sexuality.

Patrick, leaving us as he did his *Confessions*, gives us an insight into his attitude toward women and his sexuality. Noel O'Donoghue writes most movingly about this in his book on Patrick entitled *Aristocracy of Soul*. He gives a chapter of his book to exploring a little paragraph toward the end of Patrick's *Confessions*, in which Patrick writes about a "blessed Scottic maiden, nobly born, very beautiful, of adult age," whom he baptized. She gave herself as a virgin to serve the church. She has no name, so O'Donoghue calls her *Pulcherrima*, the word Patrick uses to describe how beautiful this maiden is. O'Donaghue explores why Patrick mentioned this young woman. Was he troubled by this very attractive presence? Was he tempted sexually? He may have been tempted, but it seems to O'Donoghue that there is something else happening here: Patrick's discovery of the gift of femininity to the church. For Pulcherrima gave herself as a virgin to service in the church. She voluntarily chose not to use her beauty for other ends. Yet this was not a denial of her beauty—she was not going to hide it. It was a gift for the church. O'Donoghue concludes:

> [Patrick] is deeply and sensitively open to women and womanhood, and has in himself a certain vulnerability, if not a susceptibility, which nevertheless does not take refuge in a grim and pretentious asceticism, nor yet in that neurotic fear of and contempt for the feminine which has entered so deeply into the attitudes and structures of the Christian Church in its main manifestations. In this respect he is a complete man.[9]

It seems that the Celtic Church had a wonderfully whole attitude toward human sexuality, affirming male and female, and finding both naturally expressed in the lives of their community. Interestingly, the Celt's relatively radical approach to women's ministry did not prevent them from affirming the domestic work of women. Brigid, despite all her leadership work in Christian ministry, is remembered in tradition for her "motherliness." Many Celtic prayers in the home involve invocations to Brigid. Along with Mary, the mother of Jesus, she is frequently remembered in Celtic domestic prayers. In fact, this dimension of Brigid's character was so important that in time a legend arose that she was a midwife and wet-nurse present at the birth of Christ. Thus we have prayers such as:

> I am under the shielding
> Of good Brigit each day;
> I am under the shielding
> Of good Brigit each night.
>
> I am under the keeping
> Of the nurse of Mary,
> Each early and late,
> Every dark, every light.
>
> Brigit is my companion-woman,
> Brigit is my maker of song.
> Brigit is my helping woman,
> My choicest of women, my woman of guidance.[10]

No doubt this imagery was connected with the belief that

she was a midwife to the church in Ireland. But in its devotion to Brigid, the Celtic Church found a model of one who could be both motherly and masterful. The two were not mutually exclusive or divided as they had become in other forms of European Christianity.

We find then in the Celtic Church an impressive acceptance of the feminine. It is sad to think of how we lost this following the Synod of Whitby. Had we been allowed to pursue the natural faith that the Spirit of God first breathed upon this land— a faith which had a far more just attitude toward women than existed in the church elsewhere—then we may not have had the shameful history of repression of women that we have today. We would also have had a far healthier attitude toward sexuality in general, affirming the masculine and feminine within ourselves, and within our communities.

Bible Reading

Luke 24:1–12 The women are given the honor of being the first witnesses to the resurrection of Jesus.

Questions for Reflection and Discussion

1. What is the attitude toward women in your church? Has the ministry of women been encouraged? If not, what discourages it? Spend some time speaking to the Lord about this.

2. Reflect on how you feel about your own sexuality. Do you feel affirmed by God in your femininity/masculinity? Do you feel affirmed in the community of the church?

3. Spend some time meditating on Brigid's or Hilda's community. Imagine this community bustling with life and compare it with your church. Are there aspects of the Celtic community that you would like to see in your church?

Prayer

May I abide in Christ.
May the brightness He gave Brigid lie on me.
May the delight He gave Brigid lie on me.
May the blossom He gave Brigid lie on me.

May the healings He gave Brigid lie on me.
May the calmness He gave Brigid lie on me.[11]

Notes

1. Peter Beresford Ellis, *Celtic Inheritance*, p. 20.
2. Nora Chadwick, *The Celts* (Penguin, 1971).
3. Shirley Toulson, *The Celtic Year* (Element, 1993), p. 80.
4. Mary Calvert, *God to Enfold Me* (Grail, 1993).
5. Christopher Bamford and William Parker Marsh, *Celtic Christianity, Ecology and Holiness* (Floris Books, 1986).
6. Bede, *Ecclesiastical History*, p. 245f.
7. Bede, *Ecclesiastical History*, p. 244.
8. For a novel on the life of Hilda, read Anne Warin Marshall's *Hilda* (Morgan and Scott, 1989).
9. Noel O'Donoghue, *Aristocracy of Soul*, p. 73.
10. Quoted in Esther de Waal's *The Celtic Vision*, p. 198. It is a shortened form of the original which can be found in the *Carmina Gadelica*, 111, 161–3.
11. *A St. Brigid Night Office*, St. Aidan Trust.

Chapter 11

The Power of Prayer

Patrick, Evangelist and Pastor

There is some speculation about the dates of Patrick's life and ministry. Such is the weave of historical fact and legendary tale surrounding the life of this great missionary that it is hard to know firm details of his life. However, there is a consensus that he was clearly a very great evangelist and pastor, and he is one of the few early Celtic Christians who left us a written record of his own life and ministry.

Patrick was a British Celt born sometime around the turn of the fifth century in the northwest of Britain. It was common in those days for people to go to other lands and grab a few healthy young boys to take home as slaves. And so it was that a group of Irish slave traders captured Patrick when he was sixteen and he came into the possession of a chieftain named Milch. He was put to work herding cattle in County Antrim, and here, like the Prodigal Son, he "returned with a whole heart to the Lord my God." It was on the slopes of Slemish, near Ballymeana, that Patrick experienced an extraordinary surge of prayer, as he records in his "Confession":

> But after I had come to Ireland I daily used to feed cattle, and I prayed frequently during the day; the love of God and the fear of Him increased more and more, and faith became stronger, and the spirit was stirred; so that in one day I said about a hundred prayers, and in the night nearly the same; so that I used even to remain in the woods and in the mountains; before daylight I used to rise to prayer, through snow, through frost, through rain, and I felt no harm; nor was there any slothfulness in me, as I now perceive, because the spirit was then fervent within me.[1]

Patrick tells us that one night, during this intense period of prayer, he had a dream that he would return home. He duly escaped and caught a boat to France where he trained as a priest. He then returned to Britain when he had a further prophetic dream. In the dream he saw a man coming from Ireland who gave a letter to Patrick entitled "The Voice of the Irish." As he read this, he heard the voice of many Irish people beckoning him to come and walk among them. This dream was his call to Ireland and, following his consecration as bishop, he arrived in 435 A.D., probably at Strandforth Lough. During the next three decades he engaged in vigorous and effective evangelistic work and, by the time he died in 461, he left behind him thousands of baptized Christians, and many communities that were blossoming into life.

The prayer life of the early Celtic Church is worthy of the admiration of Christians of every tradition. In this church you find contemplative hermits leading austere lives of fasting and contemplative prayer. You also find pentecostal enthusiastic prayer. Perhaps the Celtic Church, more than any other, was true to St. Paul's exhortation to the Ephesians, to "pray in the Spirit on all occasions with all kinds of prayers and requests." (Eph. 6:18 NIV)

The Hermit and the Ascetic Life

Possibly the clearest example of the vital place of prayer was the life and ministry of the hermit. It is no surprise that a church so closely connected with the Desert Fathers should see such a flourishing of eremetical life. St. Anthony, the first and most renowned Desert Father, who lived to be over one hundred years old despite his austere life in the Egyptian desert, was greatly loved and admired by the Celtic Church. The ancient high crosses of Monasterboice in Ireland are carved with two saints—Anthony and Paul of Thebes, both Desert Fathers. The Celtic Church found such people a great inspiration and, though the climate of northern Europe was very different from the hot deserts of Egypt, the principles of Desert spirituality could be applied.

Martin Palmer writes:

> In many parts of Ireland, Wales, and Scotland you can find tiny chapels or the remains of hermitages in the most remote and desolate places. Quite often these places will bear names such as Dysart, Disserth, or the like. These words are all corruptions of the word desert. And they were so called because in the Celtic monastic tradition, to go to a remote place for spiritual retreat was to go into the desert. The idea of going to the desert is a direct link back to the Coptic monks.[2]

Some would seek these deserts for short periods of time. For example, as we have seen, it was the custom of Celtic bishops to go to a "desert" to fast and pray during Lent. Thus Cuthbert and his successor on Lindisfarne, Eadbert, would go to the island now called "Cuddy's Isle," a little tidal island a few yards from Lindisfarne. Here they, and many after them, would spend short or long periods of time in prayer and quietness. For Cuthbert it was the call to a more prolonged solitary life. He eventually felt called to go to an island further out to sea, Farne Island, which Aidan had used as a place for retreat. He lived on this island for almost ten years before he was persuaded to return to the mainland and become a bishop. Bede tells us that Cuthbert went to Farne Island for "solitary contemplation and silence." He was not alone all the time, but had regular visits from the Lindisfarne community. Members of the community would come over to help him build his dwelling and his chapel, and to prepare the land so that he could grow his own food. Cuthbert actually became more and more remote on Farne Island, eventually building a high-walled, open-roofed dwelling for himself, and even blocking up the window so that when monks did come to visit him, he could not see their faces. All he saw in his last years on Farne Island was the sky, as he kept his gaze to heaven.

Such asceticism was common in the Celtic Church, though we do not have many records of some of the more bizarre forms of ascetic behavior that were taking place in the East. The ascetic life, lived out in some remote and fairly hostile places, not only encouraged a sense of doing battle in the wilderness and following the example of our Lord, but the close proximity to the forces of nature also had the effect of quickening the spirit in prayer. Patrick's experience of praying in the hostility of winter is an example of this. His contact with the cold frosts made him more sharply aware of the cold hearts of his captors, and the contrasting compassionate and warm heart of God. Cuthbert's hours praying in the cold sea may seem absurd to those who are accustomed to saying their prayers in the comfort of a fireside armchair, but there is no doubt that the experience fueled a fire within him which probably literally warmed him up. There have been a number of testimonies of Christians who were held captive in Siberian camps being enabled to pray in the coldest of conditions yet remain warm.

This kind of asceticism is a form of fasting. Not everyone in the Celtic communities lived ascetic lives, but all would regularly fast. Asceticism widened the arena of fasting to include celibacy and the withdrawal from human comforts. Fasting has the effect of making the spirit more alert to God, and there is no doubt that Cuthbert and others were very spiritually sensitive.

When he eventually left Farne Island, Cuthbert's place was taken by Ethelwald. Such places became sanctified by holy people, and they became like spiritual watchtowers. If one hermit left, another would come and take his or her place, standing guard in prayer.

In our utilitarian age it is very had to understand the purpose of the hermit life. We think of Cuthbert, this gifted evangelist and teacher, cutting himself off from his fellow creatures, denying himself all the good things of this world. And yet the Celtic Church, with all its love for creation and life, had no difficulty in accepting this ministry. I think the only way of understanding it is to see this ministry as representative. The Celtic Church knew that prayer and devotion to God had to be at the heart of its life if it was to effectively witness to God. The hermit was to some degree living out fully what most Christians could live out only partially. It was essential that some from the community lived out this life for the sake of the community, and indeed for the sake of the wider community. The hermit gave a kind of anchor to a church, which could easily have become over-busy and was, no doubt, tempted with materialism in the same kind of ways that the church is today. It is interesting to read about Fursey, who became immensely popular when he preached in Ireland. Bede tells us that "he could no longer endure the crowds that thronged him," so he abandoned all he possessed, including his ministry, left Ireland, and came to East Anglia. There he built a monastery, but again, in the face of rising success, he withdrew and lived the rest of his life as a hermit.

The church of today would do well to consider this vital aspect of the life of the Celtic Church. We all too easily give in to the seduction of business, measuring our value by our usefulness rather than our being. I am deeply grateful to one hermit I know whom I correspond with occasionally, and whom I have once visited in his little caravan in a field. I find it deeply reassuring to know he is there, as a protest movement in the face of the relentless busyness of so much of our church life. Why do we consider it to be of greater value to have our bishops and clergy attending committees and meetings throughout Lent, rather than their spending six weeks in contemplative prayer? The Celtic attitude, illustrated so aptly by the life of the hermit, deeply challenges our values.

All Kinds of Praying

The Celtic hermit would have engaged in all kinds of praying. There were times of aggressive (and probably noisy) battle prayer when the hermits engaged forces of darkness in their praying (as we shall see in Chapter 13). But they also knew the prayer of silence and stillness, which was the foundation of the contemplative life so treasured by the Celtic Church.

The hermit was never thought to be in isolation. He or she was part of the monastic community. Cuthbert, therefore, when he was on Farne Island, was still seen to be very much part of the community. In the monastic communities, there was a regular rhythm of prayer and worship. Aidan soon set up a pattern of prayer and worship on Lindisfarne that became an easy-to-follow example for all. Bede writes, "Many devout men and women of that day were inspired to follow his example, and adopted the practice of fasting until None on Wednesdays and Fridays throughout the year, except during the fifty days of Easter."[3]

They clearly saw themselves as having an intercessory responsibility for the nation. After a victory against the ever threatening Penda, King Oswy gave twelve grants of land where, as expressed by Bede, "heavenly warfare was to take the place of earthly." This land became the home of a monastic community whose job it was to make constant intercession for the peace of the nation. To turn a battle site into a place of prayer was typical of the Celtic desire to heal the land, to turn darkness to light.

The Celtic Church seems to have been at ease with formal prayer and they kept the offices in their communities. But we have many records of more spontaneous, charismatic prayer. One Epiphany, Cuthbert found himself with a couple of brothers on an island on the coast of Scotland. The weather turned bad and they could not get off the island. With no food or water the situation was serious. Bede relates Cuthbert's wonderful response to the crisis:

> "Why do we remain listless and unresourceful?" he asked. "We ought to be thinking over every possible way of saving ourselves. The land is bleak with snow, clouds lour in the sky, there is a gale raging and the sea is a fury of waves, we are dying of hunger and there is no chance of human aid. Then let us storm Heaven with our prayers, asking that the same Lord who parted the Red Sea and fed His people in the desert to take pity on us in our peril."[4]

The storms that caused the waves to pound on the rocks, stirred Cuthbert to prayer. I can imagine him standing in the waves and crying out his prayers with his great voice being carried on the gales to heaven. This wind-inspired storming of heaven was truly charismatic prayer! Needless to say it was not long before they found food and the storm settled and they made for home. Patrick's fervent prayers, must also have had a lot of energy behind them. Prayer was often quite physical. People would pray as they walked. Crossing yourself was a regular part or prayer, as was the drawing of an imaginary circle around you in one of the encircling prayers. Some prayer seems to have been very energetic.

Much of the prayer of the Celtic Church would have been spontaneous, but in time certain prayers became part of church and community rituals, and it is these where were passed down the generation and were gathered in Carmichael's *Carmina Gadelica*. Even a brief study of these prayers reveals a great respect for words, which challenges the wordiness of some church prayers today, both written and extempore. Many of these Celtic prayers are beautifully and poetically written and are designed to stir the soul and touch the heart. With the Celtic love for creation, many connect with the seasons and with all the various aspects of life in God's created order. Celtic Christians found it as natural to pray during the milking of the cow, as they did in church. In fact it was vital to feel at ease in praying while doing such mundane things as milking your cow, because if you could not do that your spiritual and earthly worlds were becoming far too separate. Thus there are prayers for getting up in the morning, for washing and dressing, for working, for resting, for meeting friends, for eating, for tidying the house, for undressing, for going to bed. In this way the Celtic Church was returning to our Jewish roots, for in Jewish spirituality there has always been a strong earthiness in prayer. David Adam's book *Power Lines*[5] is an excellent example of prayers which connect with modern-day work.

Some evangelicals will find the references to the saints difficult in Celtic prayers, but we need to remember how very important the sense of community was to the Celts and, as in Jewish tradition the community always included those loved ones who had died, for whom life had not ended, simply changed. Mary, Brigid, and the Archangel Michael are particularly popular in prayers. They all have heavenly tasks to assist our work on earth.

Celtic prayer was always deeply Trinitarian. A prayer would often involve all three members of the Trinity (see the prayer at the end of this chapter as an example). Coming into the presence of God in prayer meant coming into the presence of all three members of the Trinity, and the reference to the Three in prayer was deeply reassuring, because the pray-er would be made to think of the harmony and unity of the Trinity.

It is sad that down through the ages different ways of praying have become identified with different churchmanships and denominations. It is my conviction that God now wants to break up all of this, so that we can be a united church again, enjoying the fullness of "all kinds of praying."

Bíble Reaðíng

Mark 1:32–39 Jesus sets the pattern of finding a desert place for prayer in the face of many demands on his time.

Questíons for Reflectíon anð Díscussíon

1. How do you feel about contemplative, silent prayer? Is it your natural way of praying? Think about those times Jesus went to a desert place for peace and quiet. Try spending some time today in stillness.

2. What has been your experience of charismatic prayer? Have you engaged in "heaven storming" prayer? Why not go out for a walk on a windy day and pray as the wind stirs you. Feel the moving of the Spirit in you as you pray.

3. You might like to investigate some other Celtic forms of prayer. In the chapel at Iona it has been a tradition to have a net which has become a prayer net. When anyone says a prayer, they tie a colorful piece of wool on the net. You could do this in your home or church.

Prayer

Before a time of intercession:

*Father in heaven, Jesus came to you at the dawning of the day in a
    desert place to be still,*
Send stillness to my heart now.
Jesus, you intercede for me at the right hand of the Father,
Help me now to open my heart, mind, body, and spirit in you.
Spirit, you are the wind from heaven, that shook the upper room,
Come to me now, come as gentle breath, come as mighty wind.

Blessed Three,
I come in humility,
I come by grace,
I come with confidence,
I pray in your name,
Father, Son, and Holy Spirit.[6]

Notes

1. From *The Confession of Patrick* quoted in Noel O'Donoghue, *Aristocracy of Soul*, (DLT, 1987), p. 105.
  2. Martin Palmer, *Living Christianity* (Element, 1993), p. 69.
  3. Bede, *Ecclesiastical History*, p. 150.
  4. Bede, "Life of Cuthbert," in *The Age of Bede*, p. 57.
  5. David Adam, *Power Lines* (Triangle, 1992).
  6. General Prayers, St. Aidan Trust.

Chapter 12

Prophetic Visions
and Dreams

Fursey, and the Four Fires

F ursey (sometimes called Fursa) was born in Ireland at the end of the sixth century. Tradition has it that he was baptized by the great St. Brendan. As a child he loved reading the Scriptures and he was sent to study under Abbot Meldan on the isle Insequin in Lough Corrib, where the ruin known as Killursa (Cill Fursa) still stands today. It was not long before Fursey was involved in a very active traveling ministry, and large crowds gathered to hear him. It is clear that Fursey grew increasingly anxious about these crowds, and he retreated to a small island off the west coast of Ireland to seek God's guidance. It was here that he felt God preparing him for a new mission. Whether he knew that the king of the Angles was asking for missionaries, we do not know. But we do know that he set sail in a coracle with his two brothers and a couple of friends, either planning to travel to East Anglia, or, in Celtic fashion, simply set sail, entrusting their journey to the wind of the Spirit.

They arrived on the east coast of England in 633 A.D. to embark on their mission to the Angles. They were welcomed by King Sigebert, who had become a Christian in France. Sigebert gave Fursey a base at Burgh Castle, the site of the last fort the Romans had built before leaving Britain. Fursey spent many years there, often crossing the estuary near Great Yarmouth to bring the gospel to the people of the area now called Norfolk. Bede tells us that "inspired by the example of his goodness and the effectiveness of his teaching, many unbelievers were converted to Christ, and many who already believed were drawn to greater love and faith in him."

During this time Fursey became very ill and, over a period of days during this illness, he was given a series of extraordinary visions. Bede tells us that he "quitted his body" from sunset to cockcrow, which presumably means he was having the kind of experience Paul describes in 2 Corinthians 12. During these times he saw huge choirs of angels. He told others later that he regularly saw the souls of the departed singing, "The saints shall go from strength to strength," and

"The God of gods shall be seen in Sion." But he also saw terrible visions of evil spirits, who taunted him.

On one occasion during these days of illness and visions, he was taken by some angels high up into the sky. The angels told him to look down at the earth. As he looked down he saw a gloomy valley and four fires in the air. The angels told him that these fires were terrible desires that threatened to consume the world: falsehood, when Satan is not renounced and evil is pursued; covetousness, when worldly wealth is put before the love of God; discord, when relationships are hurt and broken; and cruelty, when the weak are robbed and defrauded. Fursey watched these fires with horror as they grew together into one terrible conflagration, and he saw great battles between warrior angels and dark demons. At one point Fursey was burnt by the fires in this vision, which left physical scars on his shoulder and jaw for the rest of his life. Fursey recovered from his illness, and the rest of his life and ministry was deeply affected by this prophetic vision. So impressed was he by it that, when he would relate the story, we are told that he would sweat profusely, even on a bitter winter's day.

The kind of prophetic vision that Fursey received was not uncommon among Celtic Christians. They were constantly expectant that God wished to show them heavenly insights that would affect their life and ministry on earth. Fursey's vision actually has a remarkable message. Today, as we survey the spiritual health of Britain, we still see the evidence of those four fires: people tampering with occultism and witchcraft and satanism spreading; the fire of materialism and consumerism destroying many lives; deep crises occurring over human relationships; and serious injustices befalling the poor and the weak. If Fursey were to be taken above Britain today, he would see the same fires burning. Our problem is that, after two hundred years of enlightenment thinking, church and secular society have lost their ability to be open to the visionary. However, there are signs that this is changing.

The Celtic Church, unencumbered with the burdens of rationalism, gave a high value to the imagination. One of the main reasons for this is that it was so in touch with creation.

The material and spiritual were not harshly divided. Bishop Richard Harris has written:

> One of the strengths of the Christian faith is the way it can hold together in one vision the physical and spiritual. The world has been created good/beautifully by God. Christ has claimed it as his own and will raise it to eternal life and light. This means that the material and the immaterial, the visible and the invisible, the physical and the spiritual interpenetrate one another.[1]

Seeing and Perceiving

One of David Adam's earlier books is called *The Eye of the Eagle*. In this book he tells us of the Celtic Church's love for St. John's gospel, the traditional symbol of which is the eagle. The eagle was much admired by the Celtic Church because it could fly higher than any other bird, and it had the sharpest eyesight. They too longed for the ability to "fly high" and have sharp eyesight to see the things of God. But their seeing was not just in the kind of dramatic vision that Fursey had. The training ground for such visions was learning to see and hear God through his creation on earth.

Jesus often communicated with his disciples through parables. He took events or principles from this world and pointed out how they communicated a deeper truth. In Matthew's gospel (13:1–17), when the disciples asked Jesus why he communicated through parables, Jesus replied by quoting from the sixth chapter of Isaiah, which describes Isaiah's wonderful vision. Here Jesus connected parable telling with vision giving. Quoting the words of God to Isaiah, he said that the people to whom he would prophesy had a serious problem in seeing but not perceiving, and in hearing but not understanding. In other words, their hearing and seeing only went so far. Isaiah's hearing and seeing had gone much further, it had gone as far as heaven itself. The Celtic Church therefore had a clear grasp of the parable principle.

A modern illustration of this is the stereogram—a picture which appears to be two-dimensional, but if you look at it, focusing correctly, a three-dimensional picture appears. You can see, and then perceive a deeper, fuller picture. Dan Dychman, a pioneer in this field, writes, "The idea of stereoviewing these images is that you will be looking through the images.... You don't want to look directly at the surface of the page, but rather to gaze through the page."[2]

This is exactly what the Celts were doing as they looked at all that was painted on the pages of creation. They had learned to look *through* the page with their open imagination, and it is no wonder that, as a result, they were given Isaiah-type visions.

As we study the Celtic Church, we find a people who were intuitively very aware, not only of seeing and perceiving, but also of hearing all kinds of signals from heaven. Cuthbert was someone who had this imaginative ability to see with the eye of the eagle. A reading of Bede's *Life of Cuthbert* introduces a man whose ministry was steeped in prophetic visionary activity. As a child he was prophesied to by an infant, which seems to have indicated that prophecy was to play an important part in his ministry. His much loved prior, Boisil, prophesied to him as they unfolded the gospel of John, the eagle, together. Boisil was given the eagle eye into Cuthbert's life. Not long after Boisil's death, Bede writes of Cuthbert, "Meanwhile the man of God began to grow strong in prophecy, foretelling the future and revealing to those near him events that were happening elsewhere."[3]

After his ten years on Farne Island, this ability seems to have been all the sharper. While on Farne Island, he was in touch with Hilda's successor, Aelfflaed,[4] the sister of King Ecgfrith. She had a deep affection for Cuthbert and, on one occasion, she fell sick and longed for him to come and pray for her. Not long after the wish was expressed, someone arrived with a linen cincture sent by Cuthbert. The cincture, blessed by Cuthbert, became the means of God's healing for Aelfflaed. After two days of wearing it, she was up and well. The reason Cuthbert had sent this gift was because "her wishes had been made known to him by heavenly means." In charismatic circles nowadays, it would be said that Cuthbert had been given a word of knowledge.

Some time after this, Aelfflaed became very concerned

about her brother who, though he was a Christian, was beginning to become more aggressive in his desire to seek further land for the Northumbrians. She pleaded with Cuthbert for a meeting. Cuthbert agreed to meet her at the monastery on Coquet Island, a halfway point between Whitby and Farne Island. When they met, she begged him to tell her what was going to become of her brother. "I know you can tell me," she said, "for the spirit of prophecy is strong in you." Cuthbert was reluctant to give her a straight answer, but knowing that the king would be dead within a year, he intimated this to her. Cuthbert also had knowledge that Aldfrith, who was currently on the island of Iona, would succeed the king.

That autumn Cuthbert was persuaded by King Ecgfrith to leave his beloved Farne Island and become the bishop of Lindisfarne. He was consecrated at York on Easter Day, 26 March 685. But Ecgfrith was on the warpath again, and was pushing north into Scotland. During his forays north, Cuthbert went to Carlisle on his first episcopal visitation. The queen was there awaiting the outcome of a fierce battle that her husband was engaged in at Nechtansmere. Cuthbert knew that his prophecy to Aelfflaed was nearing fulfillment. On the Saturday afternoon, 20 May 685, Cuthbert and the queen were being taken around the city wall to see a remarkable Roman fountain that had been built into it. Cuthbert suddenly felt very disturbed in his spirit, and he partially collapsed, leaning against the wall. With a deep sigh he said, "Perhaps at this moment the battle is being decided." A priest nearby, panicking a little, blurted out, "But how do you know this?" Cuthbert's answer is very interesting. He replied, "Do you not see how strangely disturbed the air is?" It seems that Cuthbert's eagle eye had become so clear that he could sense this national disturbance in the air. He had learned to look *through*, not just, *at* the air around him.

On the following Monday, a fugitive from the battle arrived and reported that at the very moment that Cuthbert felt the air disturbed, the king and his bodyguards had been slaughtered in the battle. Cuthbert was perhaps peculiarly gifted with a very acute prophetic sense, and Farne Island had no doubt provided an ideal training ground for this.

Dreams, the Intuitive, and Guidance

One very respected medium for communication with God
was that of dreams. As we saw in Chapter 10, it was Hilda's
mother's dream that revealed the extent of Hilda's ministry.
Caedmon's ministry in Hilda's convent came about by means
of a dream. Patrick had a number of dreams that profoundly
affected him. Noel O'Donoghue writes, "There were two
sources of light in the world of Patrick, son of Calpornius...
Holy Scripture and his own dreams."[5]

Patrick's *Confession* is a short work, but it contains seven
distinct dream narratives. It was a dream that caused him to
escape from Ireland, and it was a dream that caused him to return. It was in a dream that he engaged in a terrible moment
of spiritual battle with Satan and it was in a dream that he, in
some mystical way, saw the Holy Spirit praying with him.
Patrick was bold in speaking about his prophetic dreams, because he knew these dreams gave his ministry authority, such
was the respect in which dreams were held by the Celtic
Church. In the secular world there is a fast growing interest in
dream activity, but the church has been slow to catch up.
Hopefully we can learn to respect our dreams again, ac-
knowledging them as authentic God-given prophetic gifts.

This openness to the intuitive, together with the confident
anticipation that God delighted to communicate with his people, meant that the Celtic Church often went about its de-
cision-making process in different ways than the church of
today. Today's church is far more at ease with working par-
ties and committees than with the dangerous world of the
prophetic, which is deemed far too subjective and unreliable.
The Celtic Church was also in contrast with the Roman
Church, which was much more at ease with models of decision making taken from the structures of the Roman Empire.
The coming of Augustine to Canterbury is an excellent example of the contrasting methods of the two churches.

In 597 A.D. Augustine and forty monks arrived at
Canterbury to begin the Rome-initiated mission to the

English. The mission was successful, but after a while it became clear that the Roman Church was significantly different from the British Celtic Church. In 603 A.D. Augustine summoned some bishops to a meeting in Gloucestershire. A rather cool meeting took place, and Augustine challenged the Celtic bishops to a kind of contest to discover which church was to become the dominant church for the British, Celtic or Roman. He found a blind Englishman and he said that whoever could heal this man would "be followed by all." The British priests and bishops could not heal him, but Augustine was successful. This kind of charismatic contest would have been anathema to the Celtic Church. It did, on occasion, accept such a challenge from the pagan druids when provoked, but to engage in such a contest between Christians was totally against its values, which were to avoid all competitiveness.

The Celtic leaders were therefore very uneasy with this way of discerning God's will and asked for a further meeting. The Celts chose some bishops and leaders, most of who were from the lively community at Bangor. They went to a hermit and asked him if they should abandon their own traditions at Augustine's command. It is very interesting to observe that they put more faith in this humble hermit than they did in the Pope's bishop to the English. Such was their confidence in the hermit's prophetic gift that they dared to ask him such a straight question. For had he said "yes," it would have meant a massive upheaval for the British Church.

However, he replied neither "yes" nor "no." Bede records for us that he answered, "If he [Augustine] is a man of God, follow him." Understandably the bishops asked how they could know this. The hermit replied that the clue would be in Augustine's humility. He said, "If he rises courteously as you approach, rest assured that he is the servant of Christ and do as he asks. But if he ignores you and does not rise, then, since you are in the majority, do not comply with his demands." This, then would be the clue.

The British leaders then went to Augustine, ready to see the signal that the hermit had alerted them to. Sadly, far from showing any humility, Augustine sat firmly in his chair and, in a fairly confrontational way, began trying to put the Celtic bishops in their place. But the Celtic bishops were not to be moved. Their hermit had spoken prophetically and, as far as they were concerned, Augustine had proved that he was not worthy to be archbishop of Canterbury, so they could not respect him as such.[6]

We may judge the Celtic leaders as simplistic, and it is certainly unfortunate that a healthier relationship with Augustine could not have been established, but the point is that they had learned to deeply respect the ministry of the hermit who, on their behalf, had given years to listening to God. They were not interested in charismatic competitions of power. Neither were they impressed by fine oratory, which Wilfrid was later to use at the Synod of Whitby. For them, the all important thing was humility, and for all the strengths of the Augustinian mission, which were many, it seems it did not have the kind of meekness that was such an inspiring feature of the Celtic Church. As the Celtic Church declined in these lands, that openness to the prophetic gifts of the Spirit of God was mostly lost. As we seek to rediscover this gift at every level of church life, from local to national, we would do well to make sure we invest in the meekness that made the gift so effective in the early Celtic witness.

Bible Reading
Isaiah 6:1–10 Isaiah is given vision to see behind the curtain to behold the things of heaven.

Questions for Reflection and Discussion
1. How do you listen to God? Have you ever had a vision? Think of ways of developing the ability to see and perceive, to hear and understand.

2. Do you record your dreams? Do you feel there have been times when God has spoken to you in a dream? Ask him to open your dream life to his Spirit, so that he may communicate with you in this way.

3. How does your church make decisions? Is there an openness to prophetic insight? Is prophecy encouraged?

Prayer

From all that is false and flirts with evil:
Good Lord, deliver us.
From the love of riches and from greed and envy:
Good Lord, deliver us.
From insensitive words and from discord and strife:
Good Lord, deliver us.
From manipulation and from abuse of others:
Good Lord, deliver us.

Watching and praying, we draw near to you, High King of the Universe. We glimpse your awesome Presence in the gleaming pools, in the gentle coves, in storm and thunder, and in the stillness of the night. Reveal to us the mysteries of heaven; rebuke us for our wretched ways; and bring us to the place of holiness. Amen.[7]

Notes

1. Richard Harris, *Art and the Beauty of God* (Mowbray, 1993), p. 87.

2. Dan Dychman, *Hidden Dimensions* (Limited Editions, 1994), p. 5.

3. Bede, "Life of Cuthbert," in *The Age of Bede*, p. 57.

4. Bede, "Life of Cuthbert," in *The Age of Bede*, ch. 23–27.

5. Noel O'Donoghue, *Aristocracy of Soul*, p. 11.

6. Bede's *Ecclesiastical History*, p. 104ff.

7. *A Pattern of Worship for St. Fursey's Day*, St. Aidan Trust.

Chapter 13

The Spiritual Battle
against Evil

Illtyd, Founder of the Welsh Church

Many would regard Illtyd as the founder of the Welsh Church. He was born around 425 A.D. and was apparently a Breton, though some traditions say he was born near Brecon in Wales. We are informed by one writer that he was by descent a "most wise Magus Druid and a fore-knower of future events." He was also extremely intelligent and excelled in rhetoric, math, and philosophy. After his conversion, he became a very fine Old and New Testament scholar. But his early passion seems to have been for fighting. He was a Celtic warrior through and through and legend has it that he was one of King Arthur's knights. He fought for the Celts against the invading Saxons and, by all accounts, was a devoted and courageous warrior.

His unusual name comes from the Latin *Ille ab omni crimine tutus,* meaning "the one safe from all evil." His name was prophetic, for Illtyd was soon to be fighting, not against flesh and blood, but against principalities and powers of evil. According to the story, he moved from Arthur's army to Glamorgan to fight for King Paulinus. Paulinus was so impressed by Illtyd that he made him chief over his army. On one occasion, Illtyd took some of his soldiers hunting in a forest. Illtyd became separated from the rest of the group, who came across a small hut in the forest that was occupied by the old hermit, Cadoc. The hermit was living a quiet life after many years of Christian service in Ireland, Scotland, England, and Wales during which he founded a number of monasteries. But all this meant nothing to the pagan soldiers, who forced him to cook them a meal and then delighted in taunting the old man, telling obscene stories and jokes in an attempt to upset him. Eventually Illtyd turned up and was appalled to see the way his soldiers were treating Cadoc. He drove them out of the old man's hut and fell on his knees, begging forgiveness. Illtyd knew he was forgiven as the old man embraced him, and he went back to the palace.

During the night, Illtyd began to reflect on his life. Cadoc's life was in such contrast to his own. Eventually he fell asleep and had a dream that an angel came to him and said, "Until now you have been a knight serving mortal kings; from now on I want you to be a knight in the service of an immortal king, the King of all Kings." When he awoke in the morning, he was in no doubt that he now wanted to fight in God's army against the dark powers of Satan, and to no longer fight against other men. So he took off his armor and sword, crept from the palace, and walked to the coast where he found a sheltered valley near the beach. Here he embarked on a hermit life. He built himself a hut and spent long hours in prayer, now battling with the powers of darkness. It was not long before others joined him, including the king's own son, whom Illtyd educated. In time, this little community grew to a large monastic school called Llanilltud Fawr, a monastery that trained David, Samson, Gildas, and many other evangelists and teachers for Wales and beyond. He died in 505 A.D.

The world of demons and angels has always been very real to Celtic Christians. As we have seen, the Celtic view of creation was that it is essentially good. However, it was also seen as being invaded and menaced by evil spirits. The Celtic Church was aware of these spirit beings, usually not because they saw them with their physical eyesight, but because they had such an open imagination. They were able to see what Noel O'Donoghue refers to as the "imaginal world," the world that is perceived through intuitive awareness, rather than one that is experienced through scientifically verifiable senses. It has to do with the whole area of spiritual discernment. One of the gifts of the Spirit identified by St. Paul in his list in 1 Corinthians 12 is that of the discerning of spirits. It is a gift that the church today finds hard to use because, on the whole, we have not been used to operating in this kind of way, and we have a deep suspicion of anything that is too subjective. But the Celtic Church saw such gifts as not only being useful, but indeed vital for its life and ministry. It is very important for the church, in this post-Enlightenment era into which we are entering, to become familiar with the Celtic Church's understanding of spirits.

Noel O'Donoghue writes, "It is because we have lost the faculty of attunement to the region these beings inhabit that we are all too easily persuaded by certain scholars that these beings are no more than imaginary or mythical."[1]

Increasingly the Christian Church in the West is becoming open to the reality of an angel/demon realm and this faculty of attunement, which has always been so strong in the intuitive Celtic Church, is not being treated with such disdain. Of course, in many parts of the world where the church is growing rapidly, there is a relaxed acceptance of this angel/ demon region, and they find our skepticism very strange. Bishop Graham Dow, in his helpful booklet on deliverance ministry, writes:

> It is only the so-called developed Western countries which have difficulty with belief in evil spirits. The majority of the world is quite used to understanding them as part of reality. The question there is not "Do they exist?" but "Who has power over them?" The dean of a Chinese theological college, visiting the diocese of Coventry in a Mission in Partnership exercise in 1988, roared with laughter when I told him that most English clergy do not believe in evil spirits. We should be open to the possibility that the rest of the world is right in its perception of the way things are.[2]

It is all too easy to read this dimension of early Celtic literature and regard the stories of angels and demons as quaint medieval fantasy. For the Celtic saints, as for many Christians in the developing world today, this region is one of reality and not fantasy, and a proper appreciation of spiritual warfare is essential for an understanding of Celtic Christian spirituality.

If we look at the life of Cuthbert, we find a man for whom the battle was very real. While he was at Melrose, he was frequently out on preaching trips. On one such occasion, a huge crowd gathered to hear him and while he was speaking, Cuthbert became aware that "the ancient enemy, the devil, was present, come to hinder his work of salvation." Bede tells us that Cuthbert then exhorted the crowd to be on their guard against the devil's attacks, for Cuthbert explained, "he has a thousand crafty ways of harming you." Cuthbert was under no illusion that the enemy was real and dangerous. But Cuthbert also was utterly confident of the power of God.

There was no dualism in his thinking.

As Cuthbert continued to preach, the devil sent down "mock fire" to a nearby house. Bede relates:

> Sheets of flame, fanned by the wind, seemed to sweep through the whole village, and the noise of their cracking rent the air. Cuthbert managed, with outstretched arms, to restrain a few of the villagers, but the rest, almost the whole crowd, leaped up and vied with each other in throwing water on the flames. But real water has no effect on phantom fire, and the blaze raged on, until through Cuthbert's prayers the father of lies fled, taking his false fire with him into the empty air.[3]

The crowd was naturally astonished, but also felt ashamed that they had not trusted Cuthbert, who had encouraged them to pray rather than pour water on the phantom flames. Bede tells us that the crowd then appreciated that "the devil did not cease for even an hour in his warfare against man's salvation." Such stories of phantom fire may seem strange to many of us in the West, but they are not that uncommon in various parts of the world today, especially where there is an especially powerful outpouring of the Holy Spirit. There is no doubt that God was working powerfully through Cuthbert and attacks such as this on his evangelistic preaching were expected. But Cuthbert took it all in his stride, and Bede recorded it all in a fairly matter-of-fact way. There is no attempt to sensationalize the story in the way that some Christian writers today tell stories of spiritual combat. This kind of warfare was seen as normal for those who wanted to follow Christ.

Cuthbert also knew the fierceness of the battle when he was on his own on Farne Island. This was probably a far harder contest, when he was alone in a place of such vulnerability. Bede tells us that, before going to Farne Island, Cuthbert lived in solitude in the outer precincts of the Lindisfarne monastery. We know that he spent some time on "Cuddy's Isle." Bede writes:

> Not till he first gained victory over our invisible enemy by solitary prayer and fasting did he take it on himself to seek out a remote battlefield farther away from his fellow men.... The Farne lies a few miles to the southeast of Lindisfarne, cut off on

the landward side by very deep water and facing, on the other side, out towards the limitless ocean. The island was haunted by devils; Cuthbert was the first man brave enough to live there alone. At the entry of our soldier of Christ armed with "the helmet of salvation, the shield of faith, and the sword of the spirit which is the word of God," the devil fled and his host of allies with him.[4]

Contamination and Consecration

Because of the strong influence of the Desert Fathers, the Celtic Church saw these desert places as places of deep spiritual conflict. The precedent for this was our Lord's forty-day fast in the wilderness. In the Judaean desert Jesus fasted and prayed and was tempted by the devil. Cuthbert was following his master into the desert to wrestle, fight, and pray. As we see from Bede, Farne Island was a frightening place. It presumably had the feel of a graveyard on a dark night, and none before Cuthbert had dared go there alone. But why was this island so very infested with demons? Why should some places be particularly infected? Perhaps it had been the place of pagan sacrifices. Perhaps dark deeds of cursing had taken place there. We shall probably never know, but, as far as the Celtic Church was concerned, this island was a very dark place until Cuthbert cleansed it. Thereafter it became a hallowed place.

When you put the Celtic love for creation together with their extraordinary perceptiveness and understanding of the spirit realm, you find a view of land which is very interesting. As we have seen, land was good, but it could be contaminated. We get an insight into this view of land in the story of Cedd, who was asked by Ethelwald, son of King Oswald, to found a monastery to which he could come and pray and where his body could be buried. Cedd's job was first of all to find a good site for a monastery. Today we would probably look for a site with good amenities and with easy access, but this was not the way Cedd thought!

Cedd chose a site for the monastery among some high and remote hills, which seemed more suitable for the dens of robbers and the haunts of wild beasts than for human habitation. His purpose in this was to fulfill the prophecy of Isaiah: "In the habitation of dragons, where each lay, shall be grass, with reeds and rushes, so that the fruits of good works might spring up where formerly lived only wild beasts, or men who lived like wild beasts."[5]

Cedd's wish was to see the land redeemed as a symbol of God redeeming humankind. But he discerned that this particular area of land was not only naturally harsh, there was also a supernatural discomfort about the place brought about by "earlier crimes." We are not told what these were, but clearly some kind of human sin had contaminated this land which now had to be cleansed by the Christian priestly ministry of blessing the land. Cedd decided to give the whole of Lent to fasting and praying on the site to cleanse it. He fasted every day till sunset, except Sundays which were always feast days. Ten days before Easter, he was called away on some urgent business by the king, so, rather than let the fast be thwarted, Cedd asked his brother Cynibil to take over. By Easter, the fast was complete, and the land was considered clean and blessed. It was there that the monastery of Lastingham was established.

It is interesting to see how this attitude toward the land is emerging again today. Many people are becoming aware of actual geographical locations of spiritual darkness. Quite often this is connected to occult activity or some kind of human injustice committed centuries ago, but nonetheless, there still seems to be an infection in the ground. Confession and prayer are proving effective ways of changing this atmosphere. Peter Wagner and others are suggesting that in some regions there are powerful demonic forces which they call "territorial spirits." While there is some discussion about this term, there is a growing agreement that regions can contain a particular spiritually oppressive atmosphere. The converse is also true, in that some places feel especially blessed, very often places which have been soaked over the centuries in Christian prayer.

Warfare and Protection

With this keen sense of awareness of good and evil in the

world, the Celtic Church engaged actively not only in prayers of blessing, but also in prayers of protection.

Patrick was very aware of the need for protection following a sinister and frightening dream that he records in his *Confession*:

> But the same night while I was sleeping and Satan greatly tempted me, in a way which I shall remember as long as I am in this body. And he fell upon me like a huge rock, and I had no power in my limbs, save that it came to me into my mind, that I should call out "Helias." And in that moment I saw the sun rise in the haven' and while I was crying out "Helias" with all my might, behold the splendor of that sun fell upon me, and at once removed the weight from me. And I believe I was aided by Christ my Lord, and His Spirit was then crying out for me.[6]

The experience left Patrick in no doubt that the spiritual battle was real. It also left him in no doubt of the power of Christ and the Holy Spirit.

The story goes that Patrick was involved in a Mount Carmel kind of contest with the pagan druids and king of Tara, a center of witchcraft and darkness. After this victorious encounter, Patrick is said to have written the famous "St. Patrick's Breastplate." Whether he was the author or not, the prayer is certainly early and is consistent with Patrick's life and ministry. It is a glorious prayer that rejoices in the power of the Holy Trinity to protect us:

> I arise today,
> Through a mighty strength, the invocation of the Trinity,
> Through belief in the threeness,
> Through confession of the oneness
> of the Creator of Creation.[7]

The whole prayer is quite wonderful and includes some fairly specific prayers of protection against "Satan's spells and wiles," and includes references to such things as "wizard's evil craft," "poisoned shaft," and other well known devices used by those involved in witchcraft to attack Christians. Right after this part of the prayer comes the beautiful Christ-centered prayer which rises majestically as a triumphant peak:

Christ be with me, Christ within me,
Christ behind me, Christ before me,
Christ beside me, Christ to win me,
Christ to comfort and restore me.
Christ beneath me, Christ above me.
Christ in quiet, Christ in danger,
Christ in hearts of all that love me,
Christ in mouth of friend and stranger. *(Alexander's version)*

Such a prayer as Patrick's was often called a *lorica* prayer, which means "breastplate," picking up the imagery used by St. Paul in Ephesians 6:14. There are many of these prayers in the *Carmina Gadelica,* and they reflect the Celtic Church's awareness of our need for protection. Some of these prayers took the form of "encompassing" prayers, during which the right finger of the right hand would be extended and an imaginary circle would be drawn around you while you prayed a prayer of protection. In the case of Patrick's prayer above, you would see in your mind's eye the protection of Christ around, above, beneath, and within you. The encircling prayer is often called a *caim* and is becoming increasingly popular today. David Adam, who has written a number of these *caim* prayers, writes, "There was no magic, it was no attempt to manipulate God. It was a reminder by action that we are always surrounded by God, he is our encompasser, our encircler."[8]

As we read our papers and watch our television news, we can have no doubt about the reality of evil. When we see graphic and horrible details of war-torn lands, the disfigured bodies of those suffering famine, and terrible murders committed by teenagers and even children, we know that there is a deep darkness at work in the world. As we study the Celtic Church, we discover a community of Christian people who took this darkness seriously. They developed very effective ways not only of protecting themselves from its influence, but also of delivering people and lands from the influences of evil. It was because of their combination of humility and confidence, and the fact that their spirituality was so well earthed, that they developed a well integrated and thoroughly biblical response to the presence of evil in this world.

Bible Reading
Ephesians 6:10–20 Paul gives practical advice on how to resist the devil.

Questions for Reflection and Discussion
1. What is your view of spiritual warfare? How does the Celtic approach to evil compare with your own view?

2. Have you ever had experiences like those of Patrick? Have you ever been to places that have seemed "spooky?" Do you know why they feel this way? Have you been to places that have a good atmosphere and feel blessed? Why do you think they feel good?

3. Find time to take a walk in your neighborhood. Ask the Holy Spirit to give you a gift of discernment, so that you can be open to sensing good places to bless and bad places to pray about. Be open to the possibility of God taking you into a season of prayer and fasting for unhappy places in your neighborhood.

Prayer
In the midst of dark powers,
We magnify the greatness of heaven.

In the midst of foul deeds,
We magnify the greatness of heaven.

In the midst of fearful thoughts,
We magnify the greatness of heaven.

In the midst of a blighted land,
We magnify the greatness of heaven.

In our time of need,
We magnify the greatness of heaven.

We praise you, Lord of earth and heaven,
We magnify you on earth as in heaven.[9]

Notes

1. Noel O'Donoghue, *The Mountain Behind the Mountain*, p. 23.

2. Graham Down, "Those Tiresome Intruders," *Grove Pastoral*, no. 41: p. 4.

3. Bede, "Life of Cuthbert," *The Age of Bede*, p. 59.

4. Bede, "Life of Cuthbert," *The Age of Bede*, p. 66.

5. Bede, *Ecclesiastical History*, p. 181.

6. Noel O'Donoghue, *Aristocracy of Soul*, p. 106.

7. Better known is C.F. Alexander's translation, "I bind unto myself today the strong name of the Trinity." Both versions are given in David Adam's *The Cry of the Deer*. His book is based on Patrick's prayer which was sometimes called, "The Cry of the Deer," following the legend that after Tara, Patrick turned into a deer and ran free.

8. David Adam, *Tides and Seasons* (Triangle, 1989), p. 105.

9. *A Morning Office in Celtic Tradition Suitable for Michaelmas and Thursdays*, St. Aidan Trust.

Chapter 14

The Divine Restlessness
of the Wild Goose

Brendan, Abbot of Clonfert

B rendan was born around 486 A.D. near Tralee in southern Ireland and he lived to be over ninety years old. The Christianity that Patrick and Brigid had spread through Ireland meant that almost every local community had become connected with a monastic settlement. It was clear that Brendan had a special calling on his life. Before he was born, Brendan's mother dreamed that her breast was full of pure gold. On the night of his birth, Erc, the local bishop, saw the village "all in one great blaze" with angels in shining white garments all around it. When he realized that they were heralding the birth of this special child, Erc took great care of him, teaching him the Bible as he grew. In due course Brendan was ordained and became a monk.

He became one of the "Twelve Apostles of Ireland," as they were called. These were twelve men who were pupils of Finian of Clonard. It was the custom for Christian leaders to choose twelve disciples, following the pattern of Jesus. They would mentor these twelve, training them for Christian service. Finian's twelve included not only Brendan, but also Ciaran of Clonmacnoise, Brendan of Birr, and the famous Columba who eventually went to Iona.

Brendan became abbot of Clonfert, a large monastery in central Ireland. But there was restlessness in him and he was deeply infected by the Celtic spirit of adventure. He spent one Lent on top of a high mountain on the southwest tip of Ireland, above Bantry Bay, fasting and praying and looking out over the vast Atlantic. He could see the rocks of Skellig Michael, where brave monks lived an austere life in their beehive huts which still exist today. Brendan was impressed by them, but he did not want to live on an Island. He wanted to discover islands beyond the horizon. He sensed the unfurling wings of the Wild Goose, the Celtic symbol of the Holy Spirit, urging him to spread his own wings and travel to far off lands, not only with a desire to spread the gospel, but with a mystical quest to seek glimpses of Paradise. He had met travelers before who had encountered such places on earth, and he had become gripped with this longing. So sure was he that this was a call of God, that he returned to his community and chose fourteen monks to travel with him. He said to them, "My beloved fellow soldiers in the spiritual war: I beg your help, because my heart is set upon a single desire. If it be God's will, I want to seek out the Island of Promise of which our forefathers have spoken."

Thus it was that Brendan and his fourteen companions built their simple coracle and set out into the Atlantic, allowing the wild wind of the Spirit to take them where it would. The account of their travels is recorded in *The Voyage of Brendan*, which became an immensely popular book in the Middle Ages. It was no doubt highly embellished but, behind the parables and hyperboles, you discover a group of wonderfully open travelers who discovered small island communities of monks, encountered the wonders of icebergs and great whales, and traveled vast distances in their fragile coracle, quite possibly discovering America eight centuries before Christopher Columbus.

According to legend, Brendan did find his island of Paradise, but was told not to stay there because he would only spoil it! After several years of traveling, he returned to Ireland. After a very long life, he embarked on his final journey, the journey of death in 575 A.D., requesting that his body be buried at Clonfert, which was now a community numbering some three thousand brothers.

Although *The Voyage of Brendan* is embellished, the great spirit of adventure that was so much part of early Irish Christianity was clearly the inspiration behind that extraordinary journey. The story is a delightful integration of a love for creation and a longing for the spiritual reality of Paradise. On one occasion, after sailing for months in the north Atlantic without seeing anything, Brendan and his companions came across an iceberg. It was the first time they had seen one, and did not know that such things existed. Brendan gazed up at it. It was so high he could hardly see the top, and he could see that it plunged deep into the sea. It was clearly a large iceberg, and they found a tunnel that they could sail through. The writer describes it: "It was the color of silver and seemed harder than marble. The column itself was of pure crystal." Brendan was delighted to spend time with this extraordinary crystal island and exhorts his fellow travelers, "let us inspect the wonders of God, our Maker." They spent the whole day inspecting and measuring this phenomenon.[1]

This story reveals the Celtic travelers' delight of God's creation, which was one of their driving forces. They deeply desired to discover more of the wonders of creation. They experienced God as wonderful, and the wonders of creation led them on to the discoveries of the unseen wonders of Paradise.

The Celtic Church was very alert to the activity of the Holy Spirit, who was so involved in creation. They chose the symbol of the wild goose for the Spirit because, having studied this bird, they saw in it so much of the life and work of the Spirit.

Patrick and the Spirit

Patrick, whose influence was so strong in Ireland, had a strong appreciation of the presence and activity of the Holy Spirit. The Celtic Church had close associations with the Eastern Church, which has always had a "high doctrine" of the Holy Spirit. One of the points of dispute between the Eastern and Western Churches has been over the inclusion in the Creed of the word *filoque*, which means "and the Son." The Western Church describes the Spirit as proceeding from the Father *and the Son*. The Eastern Church felt this was subordinating the Spirit beneath the Son, and opted for the Creed to read simply, "proceeding from the Father." It may seem a doctrinal detail to us today, but experience has shown that the Eastern Orthodox churches have always had a high expectation of the activity and gifts of the Holy Spirit among them. Patrick eagerly picked up this love for the Holy Spirit, which is evident in his *Confession*. Noel O'Donoghue writes: "The Confession of Patrick is animated from beginning to end by the Holy Spirit, who is named as the Spirit (11, 43, 46) the Spirit of God (33), the Spirit of the Living God (11), the Spirit of the Father (20).... A more careful reading of the text shows that the Spirit initiates the whole process of Patrick's conversion and sanctification."[2]

One of the most intimate experiences of the Spirit that Patrick had is described in his *Confession* as he recounts one of his extraordinary dreams:

> And again I saw Him praying in me, and He was as it were within my body, and I heard him above me, that is above the inner man, and there He was praying mightily with groanings. And meanwhile I was stupefied and astonished, and pondered who it could be that was praying in me. But at the end of the prayer He spoke as if He were the Spirit. And so I awoke, and remembered that the Apostle says, "The Spirit helps the infirmities of our prayers. For we know not what we should pray for as we ought; but the Spirit Himself asketh for us with unspeakable groanings."[3]

This is an excellent insight into Patrick's understanding and experience of the Spirit. It tells us that he had an expectation of the Spirit communicating in his dream life. Noel O'Donoghue, in commenting on this, says that this experience informs us that "the region of dreams has within it pathways along which the Holy Spirit can reach us." The dream informs us that the Spirit is not a remote and otherworldly mystical person of the Trinity. Far from it—the Holy Spirit actually enters the most intimate place of our psyche, our inner world of the unconscious. For Patrick, and the Celtic Church, the Spirit was the glorious gift of God, who visits us intimately and powerfully. In his *Confession* we find this continuous activity of the Spirit, with the charismatic gifts of 1 Corinthians 12 very much present. We find expressions of prophecy, wisdom, knowledge, discerning of spirits and faith, and, in Patrick's wider ministry, we find the Spirit working in healings and miracles. I have yet to find reference to speaking in tongues, or interpretation of tongues in Celtic literature, though it is possible that Patrick's groanings include this. I think it is very likely that the Celtic Church loved to use this gift. On the whole the gift of tongues only presents difficulties for those who are confined to a rationalistic view of the activity of God in us. For the intuitive Celt, the idea of a heavenly language, coming from the intimacy of our hearts and bypassing the logic of mind, would have been very easy to receive.

The Celtic Church practiced the ministry of Confirmation by its bishops. In the days when the Celtic fire was burning bright, these must have been great events. Bede describes for us one of Cuthbert's confirmations:

> Once when this most holy shepherd of the Lord's flock was do-ing the round of his sheepfolds, he came into a rough moun-tain area whither many had gathered from the scattered villages to be confirmed. Now there was no church nor even a place in the mountains fit to receive a bishop and his retinue, so the people put up tents for him while for themselves they made huts of felled branches as best they could. Cuthbert preached twice to the milling crowds and brought down the grace of the Holy Ghost by imposition of hands on those newly regenerated in Christ.[4]

Such was the presence of the Spirit at this outdoor con-firmation service that a young man with a wasting disease re-ceived healing. So the Spirit was seen as coming in power at the confirmation service and thereafter would be intimately involved with the believer. Once you received the Spirit in this way, you began a life of adventure, open to the leading of this Wild Goose.

Wild Goose and Adventure

In some ways, the Holy Spirit would not have had to work too hard on the Celtic peoples, because they were travelers and explorers by nature. Nonetheless, there was a real cost in-volved in pulling up roots and venturing forth, often in small rudderless coracles, at the mercy of tides, currents, and winds, which were used by the Spirit of God to take them to places of God's choice. The cost was reflected in the use of the word "martyrdom." The Celtic Church identified two kinds of mar-tyrdom. "Red" martyrdom was dying for the sake of Christ. The early Celtic Church seldom experienced red martyrdom until the coming of the Vikings, who often headed straight for Celtic communities in their raids on the country. Visitors to Iona can still go to the bay of martyrs today, the site where 68 monks were slaughtered by Norse raiders in 806. But while there were few red martyrs in the early years, there were thousands of "green" martyrs. Green martyrdom primarily had to do with a life of confession and penance, which included a voluntary giving up of normal securities. Thus, into this category came leaving a secure home to become a *perigrinatus*, "a wanderer," for the sake of Christ. Elizabeth Culling writes: "The *peregrinati* set out with no particular destination in mind, but wherever they found themselves they preached Christ and sought to live out the gospel. The 'Lives' of the saints frequently state that pilgrimage was undertaken 'for the love of God...for the name of Christ...for the salvation of souls and to attain heaven.'"[5]

This sense of martyrdom, of giving up all for the sake of Christ, is reflected in Brendan's beautiful and touching prayer:

> Shall I abandon, O King of Mysteries, the soft comforts of home? Shall I turn my back on my native land, and my face towards the sea?
>
> Shall I put myself wholly at the mercy of God, without silver, without a horse, without fame and honor? Shall I throw myself wholly on the King of Kings, without sword and shield, without food and drink, without a bed to lie on?
>
> Shall I say farewell to my beautiful land, placing myself under Christ's yoke? Shall I pour out my heart to him confessing my manifold sins and begging forgiveness, tears streaming down my cheeks?
>
> Shall I leave the prints of my knees on the sandy beach, a record of my final prayer in my native land? Shall I then suffer every kind of wound that the sea can inflict?
>
> Shall I take my tiny coracle across the wide, sparkling ocean? O King of the Glorious Heaven, shall I go of my own choice upon the sea?
>
> O Christ, will you help me on the wild waves?[6]

The *peregrinati* felt they were being obedient to Jesus' call to leave their home and family and follow him. They were also aware that their Master was one who wandered and never

had anywhere to rest his head (Matt. 8:20). He was one who
journeyed across barren wastelands, and who walked on the
wild waves. This sense of reckless traveling, brought about by
the divine restlessness within, says much to our organized
and often far-too-safe Western Church. The Celtic Church reminds us that we were made to quest and that pilgrimage is
at the heart of our Christian discipleship. David Adam explains the title of one of his books, *The Open Gate*, in this way:

> As long as we are alive, we are on the move. To become static
> is to stagnate and die. It is necessary for all living things to
> move and grow and change. Life is meant to be an adventure;
> change is a gift that we have to learn to use aright. In Celtic
> folk-tales a curse that could happen to a person was to enter a
> field and not be able to get back out of it. To be stuck in that
> place for ever. It was seen as a definite curse to be unable to
> venture or to change.... The open gate is the opposite of this. It
> is the invitation to adventure and to grow, the call to be among
> the living and vital elements of the world. The open gate is the
> call to explore new areas of yourself and the world around
> you.[7]

Not only do we have to learn to adventure, but we also
need to know the Celtic simplicity that will let go of the bag-
gage and clutter that weighs us down. Shirley Toulson speaks
of the need to let go of our "trunkfuls of preconceptions, such
badly packed, uncomfortable rucksacks of dogma, prejudice,
and projects."[8] There is a wildness about the Holy Spirit, who
is like the wind which "blows where it chooses, and you hear
the sound of it, but you do not know where it comes from or
where it goes" (John 3:8). Too many churches have wanted to
domesticate the Holy Spirit, keeping this Wild Goose caged
and "safe" by imposing rigid and controlling worship styles
on our Sunday worship (whether it be liturgical or "free"),
trapping our meetings with bureaucracy and endless reports,
and feeding our people with tragically low expectations of
what God can do, both in and through them.

As we approach the third millennium A.D., the Celtic
Church of the first millennium wonderfully and joyfully challenges us to learn once again what it means to have a carefree
spirit of adventure. The Wild Goose is certainly blowing on

our land again with renewed force. There are signs of spiritual springtime, despite the frost and ice in many parts of our church and society. Now is surely the time to become open once again to the Spirit of God, who desires to come to the most intimate places of our lives, praying, healing, and transforming us, so that we may be released to a new sense of pilgrimage and divine restlessness.

Bible Reading
Genesis 12:1–9 Abraham is called to a pilgrim life.

Questions for Reflection and Discussion
1. How do you experience the Holy Spirit in your life? Have you, like Patrick, felt the Spirit at work in or through you in your dreams? How has the Spirit changed you inside?

2. How open are you to adventure? Do you enjoy traveling? If so, what is it that you enjoy about it? Are there new adventures that God is leading you on? What risks can you take for God? What luggage holds you down?

3. How open is your church to the Wild Goose? Are there ways it needs to let go of wanting to domesticate the Spirit? What adventures do you think God is leading you as a church to embark on?

Prayer
Father, we thank you for Brendan's adventures, for Christ and his drawing together of families and friends into communities of love. Kindle in us a spirit of endless adventure and a love that forges fresh bonds of community. Amen.

A Blessing for the Journey:
Go forth with the vision of God;
Sail into the ocean of his love.
May the Sacred Three surround and sustain you,
Till they bring you to your eternal home.[9]

Notes
1. The story of Brendan's Voyage can be found in *The Age of*

Bede. The iceberg story is on p. 236f.

2. Noel O'Donoghue, *Aristocracy of the Soul*, p. 43.

3. Noel O'Donoghue *Aristocracy of the Soul*, p. 108.

4. Bede, "Life of Cuthbert" in *The Age of Bede*, p. 83.

5. Elizabeth Culling, *What is Celtic Christianity?* (Grove Books, Spirituality no. 45, 1993).

6. Robert Van der Weyer, *Celtic Fire*, p. 30.

7. David Adam, *The Open Gate* (Triangle, 1994), p. 1.

8. Shirley Toulson, *The Celtic Year* (Element, 1993), p. 120.

9. *An Office for St. Brendan's Day*, St. Aidan Trust.

Epilogue

The Woven Cord

As we explored the various strands of the Celtic Church, we have done a lot of looking back. And yet as I have written this, I felt as if I were looking forward. We are close to the turn of a millennium, the very existence of which causes us to become aware of history, to pause, and to dare to ask about the kind of world in which we will be living in the twenty-first century, and the kind of church that is required to carry the gospel to the coming generations.

Looking back at the Celtic Church gives me great heart and vision for the future, for it reminds me that God has done the impossible before. God transformed a society that was culturally confused and riddled with spiritual uncertainty and superstition, creating a group of Christian people who lived in a beatitude lifestyle that offered a radical alternative to the decadence of the collapsing Roman Empire. This group of Christian people had a faith so rooted in the Bible that they carried the word of God in their memories, reciting psalms as they walked the muddy pathways. They formed dynamic communities of men, women, and children, which were simple in lifestyle, but rich in spiritual life and love. They were a people whose hearts were gloriously set on heaven, experiencing the remarkable expressions of the power of God, but who were in every respect wonderfully down to earth, loving creation, caring for it, and seeing through it the work of God. And they knew how to pray and how to wage the spiritual battle. Their lives were utterly given to mission; they delighted to allow the Wild Goose to take them to un-evangelized places with the good news of Jesus.

The more I read about the Celtic Church, the more I am moved and humbled by it, and the more I am convinced it is speaking to us today. Not only does the Celtic Church speak to us about our church, but it also speaks about the healing between our nations. In the case of Britain and Ireland, Celtic Christianity has immense potential for healing. As we go back to the beginning and discover all that we shared in common, there is still hope for peace in Ireland, that wonderful land where the gospel first flourished so freely. Those who live there tell me of their conviction that the rediscovery of their common Christian experience prior to the divisions of the Reformation has great potential for healing. But it is much wider than Britain and Ireland.

All over the world there is again a growing tension be-tween the two approaches typified by the Roman Church on the one hand and the Celtic Church on the other. But this time the Roman is not imposing itself on the Celtic; the Celtic way is rising up in the hearts of many people to challenge the Roman ways. Simple cells of Christian life are challenging the powerful institutions; charismatic intuitive gifts of lay people are challenging the tight grip of clerical and ministerial hier-archies; personal commitment to Jesus is challenging cold nominalism; creation-affirming spirituality is challenging the little world of private piety; genuine holiness and authenticity are challenging the glitz of commercial Christianity.

But this does not mean that we should abandon the old and start a new Celtic denomination—God forbid! The Celtic way was not to abolish, but to change and transform. Instead, our quest is to see our Christian faith once again united, so that the church at every level might be renewed by the power of the Holy Spirit. And so that it may share Christ boldly and lovingly in a very needy world, in the glory of God the Father.

Of Related Interest ...

Soul-Making

The Telling of a Spiritual Journey
Edward Sellner
An intimate book telling of a time when the author faced questions
about himself, his role in life, his ambitions and his aspirations.
ISBN: 0-89622-457-0, 208 pp, $9.95 (order C-62)

Myths

Gods, Heroes, and Saviors
Leonard J. Biallas
A panoramic view of fascinating stories from people struggling to
understand their world and the mysterious beyond.
ISBN: 0-89622-290-X, 312 pp, $12.95 (order B-18)

In the Presence of Mystery

An Introduction to the Story of Human Religiousness
Michael Horace Barnes
An introduction to the story of human religiousness that goes to the
very core of religious belief and practice, ranging from preliterate to
modern culture.
ISBN: 0-89622-425-2, 344 pp, $14.95 (order B-59)

Available at religious bookstores or from

TWENTY-THIRD PUBLICATIONS
XXIII P.O. Box 180 • Mystic, CT 06355 • 1-800-321-0411